BRYAN HUNT
A Decade of Drawings

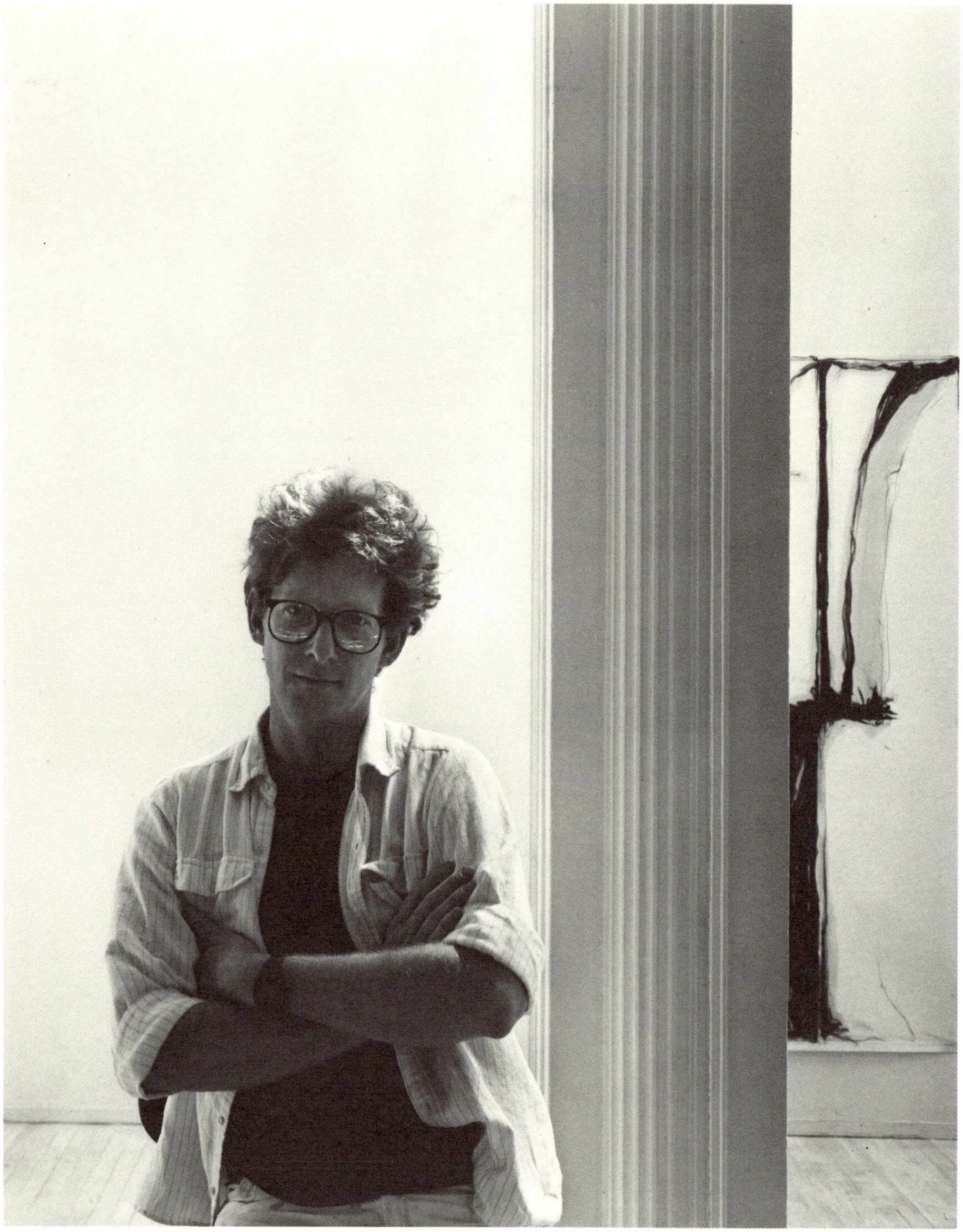

Bryan Hunt © *Arnold Newman*

BRYAN HUNT
A Decade of Drawings

November 15 - December 11, 1983

An exhibition organized by the Museum Studies Certificate Program in conjunction with The Center for Southern California Studies in the Visual Arts of The University Art Museum, California State University Long Beach

Edited by Constance W. Glenn and Jane K. Bledsoe

The Museum Studies Certificate Program

Constance W. Glenn, Director
Jane K. Bledsoe, Gloria B. Skovronsky, Faculty
Susan Taylor, Museum Studies Registrar

Library of Congress Catalogue Number: 83-21947
ISBN: 0-936270-20-9

The University Art Museum Staff

Constance W. Glenn, Director
Jane K. Bledsoe, Administrative Director
Gloria B. Skovronsky, Curator, Administrative Assistant
Sally Steiner, Curator of Education
Terry A. Chapman, Registrar
Nancy Chang, Accountant
Elizabeth R. Chalfin-Carroll,
Jamie G. Hoover, Curatorial Assistants
William David Miller, Mark Themann, Preparators

Acknowledgements

This exhibition and its accompanying video documentary, *Bryan Hunt,* would not have been possible without the assistance of many generous individuals: Joe Helman, Peter Freeman and the staff of the Blum Helman Gallery; Margo Leavin and the staff of the Margo Leavin Gallery; Roderick K. DuVall and John P. Hays, whose dedication, expertise and hours of volunteer service made the video documentary a reality; Lyn Bagdon of Long Beach Cablevision, who provided necessary equipment; Robert Finney and Isaac De La Rocha of the CSULB Radio/Television Department; and Maurice Tuchman, Gloria Wang, Richard Leddy, Bob Urhausen, Jim Wood and Kirsten Jacobs Whalen who were most helpful.

This exhibition has been supported by the CSULB School of Fine Arts, Department of Art, Instructionally Related Activities Fund, 49er Shops and Foundation. In addition a portion of the Museum's general operating support has been provided by the California Arts Council.

The 1983 Museum Studies Certificate Class would, in addition, like to thank Connie Glenn, Jane Bledsoe, Gloria Skovronsky, Jamie G. Hoover, Terry Chapman and other members of the UAM staff who shared valuable expertise and devoted countless hours to assure that the exhibition and catalogue would become a reality.

Finally the Museum and the Class are grateful to Bryan Hunt for his time, his presence, his patient cooperation and enthusiasm for our project.

1983 Museum Studies Class

C. Michelle Betty
Christie Collins
Jeff Matsuno
Shirley Pinard
Michele Redlich
Susan Taylor

The Center for Southern California Studies in the Visual Arts is a division of the Museum which deals specifically with the arts and art resources of our region and this exhibition is offered, by the students, as one in a series of Center programs.

I am personally grateful to the many individuals, both on campus and in our regional community, who have offered generous assistance and support: most especially to the lenders who have truly made the exhibition possible; to the artist, who has been unfailingly helpful and supportive; and specifically to my associates Jane Bledsoe, who guided the class on a day-to-day basis, and Gloria Skovronsky, who answered their every request or question.

We all offer our congratulations to Christie, Jeff, Michele, Michelle, Shirley and Sue and wish them every success.

Constance W. Glenn
Director

Preface

BRYAN HUNT
The Figurative Voids

The relationships created between negative and positive, between figure and ground — no matter what the mode of expression — lie at the heart of all art — old or new, figurative or abstract. Overt, compelling concern for the establishment of powerful negative/positive contrasts dominates the work of artists as diverse as Leonardo, Vermeer, Rodin, Degas, Henry Moore, Robert Motherwell, Jasper Johns, Richard Serra and Susan Rothenberg. Examples abound of the manipulation of negative space to heighten the sense of subject/form, to reinforce the illusion of three dimensionality, to provide tension between void and density, and to create pictorial ambiguity.

In the past, the witty playing of positive against negative form — questioning assumptions about perception — was apparent in Dada/Surrealist compositions, especially those of Marcel Duchamp (fig. 1). At the same time psychologists raised issues about perception with image exercises such as the vase/face and Rorschach tests, which have become classic examples of alternative choices with regard to figure/ground relationships and exemplify perceptual phenomena explored by generations of artists.[1]

Specifically, in the 1950s, creative exploitation of negative/positive ambiguity characterized the work of a number of American photographers — most notably that of Aaron Siskind (Hunt himself is an accomplished photographer). In Siskind's image (fig. 2), we are tempted to see Hunt's *The Dam,* 1980 (No. 24); while, in reality, what is seen is the depiction of space — a necessarily monocular depiction — from a conceptually similar viewpoint.

Though negative space always plays an essential role in the articulation of positive three-dimensional form in sculpture, Bryan Hunt is unique in his elaboration (in both sculpture and drawing) on the *trompe l'oeil* of artists such as Duchamp and Johns, and the vision of

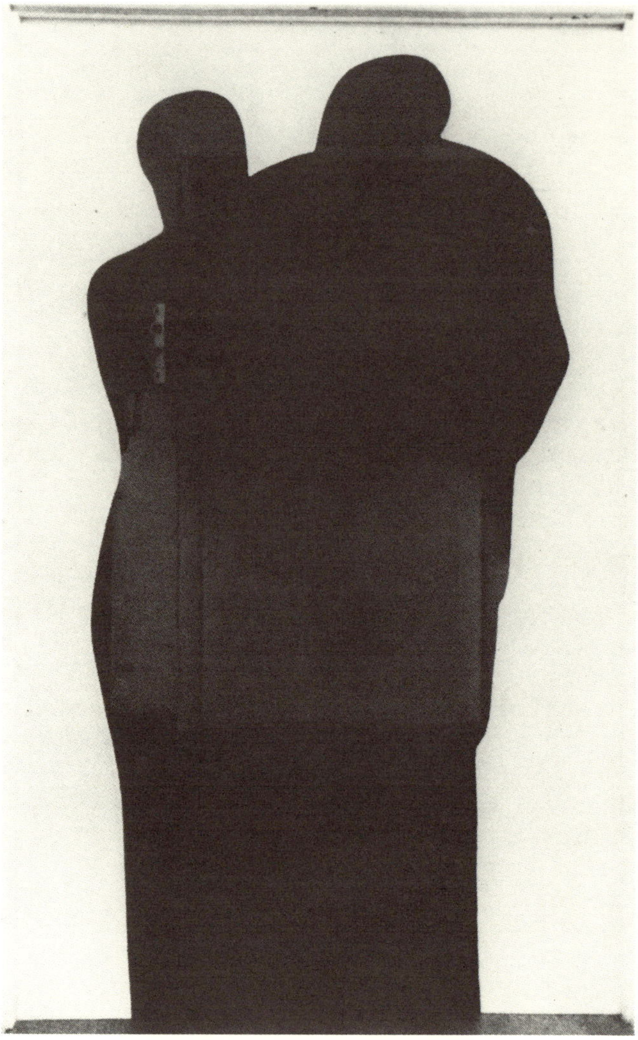

Figure 1. *Marcel Duchamp,* ***Door for Gradiva,*** *1937, glass door, original destroyed, reprinted from* ***The Complete Works of Marcel Duchamp*** *by Arturo Schwarz, courtesy of Harry N. Abrams, Inc.*

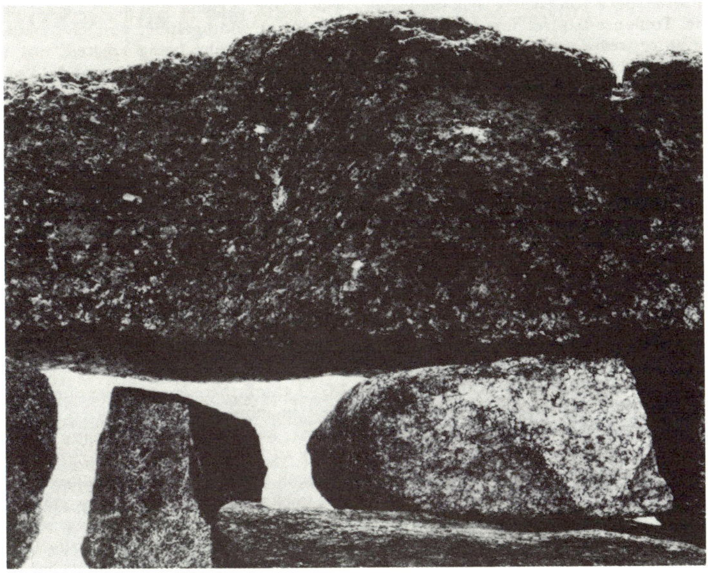

Figure 2. *Aaron Siskind,* ***Martha's Vineyard 124,*** *1954, photograph, reprinted from* ***The Print Collector's Newsletter,*** *July-August 1973.*

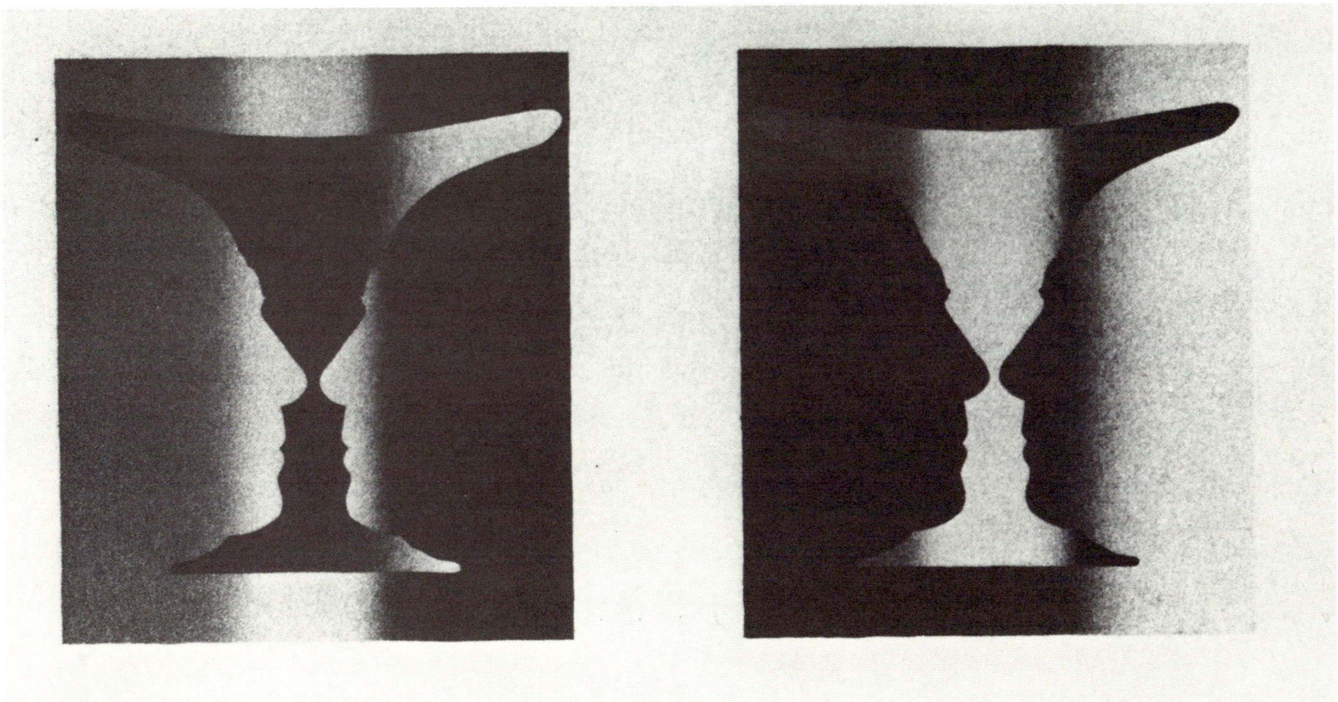

Figure 3. *Jasper Johns,* ***Cups 4 Picasso,*** *1972, lithograph from four plates printed on a hand-fed, offset proofing press, 22x32, ed. 39, U.L.A.E., reprinted from* ***Jasper Johns: Prints 1970-1977*** *by Richard S. Field, copyright ©1978, by permission of Wesleyan University Press.*

Siskind, using positive forms to create specific figurative references in the negative (fig. 3). His familiar "falls" define or outline exaggerated details from Classical art and architecture — caryatids, frontal or bisected views of upper torsos, reclining figures, slender amphoras. The images created in expressionistically worked bronze (sculpture), or dense black graphite (drawing), seem, at first, to be the apparently abstract "subjects." Prolonged observation, however, gives up subtle, but by no means concealed, references to Classical figuration. New figurative images are embodied in the voids of the forms abstracted from nature.

Once the contours of the "falls" are seen as the extremities of all manner of elements derived from Classical ornament, a tension is established between the two "subjects" — the one the eye immediately accommodates and the one intellect insists is equal. The mental exercise is akin to the old half-full, half-empty game. But the ambiguity — heightened by the romantic expressionism embodied in the surfaces and marks — is what keeps the work on edge, what provides the viewer with unexpected rewards.

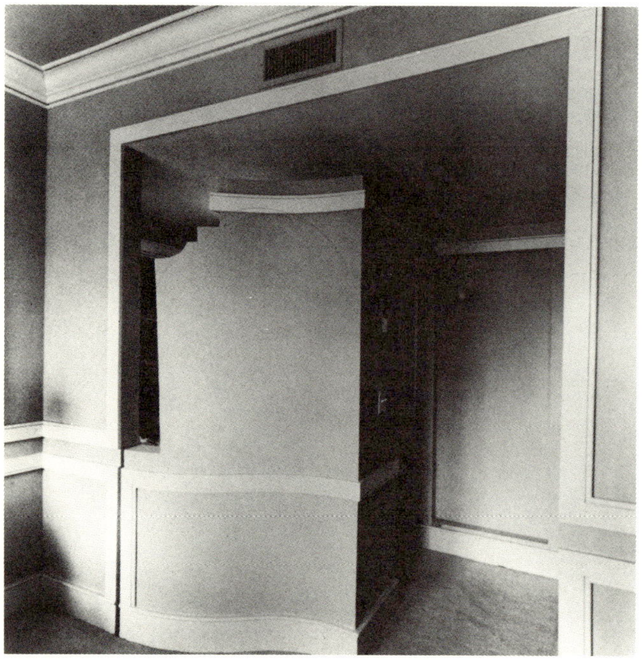

Figure 4. *©Robert A.M. Stern: "A classical column appears as a negative silhouette." Reprinted from* ***Ornamentalism,*** *by Robert Jensen and Patricia Conway, courtesy of Clarkson N. Potter, Inc.*

Hunt's treatment of space, rooted in the Conceptual art of the late sixties and early seventies, is as closely related to Post-Modern architecture as it is to contemporary painting and sculpture, although it follows loosely, in ideology, in the tradition of sculptural environments created by artists as distantly related as George Segal and Bruce Nauman.

"I happen to need," Segal has said, " . . . my own peculiar combination of hard, harsh, austere architecture, plus some kind of softness, gentleness, roundness or voluptuousness. It's my own kind of balance . . . .[2] I am trespassing on architecture too . . . I've controlled travel through space . . . I've set up my sculpture as interruptions in space and composed like an architect . . . ."[3]

The excitement, the "strength and originality," of Hunt's work (and that of the Post-Modern architects, fig. 4) lies in his ability to control travel through space and "to keep contradictions alive and explicit in the forms created . . . ." These forms play with "elements of the Classical orders . . . [and] can be seen as direct references to nature . . . its colors, shapes and rhythms . . . ."[4] In addition, particular contradictions — such as explicit allusions to monumental form — are enhanced by the introduction of an utterly human scale. Neither Hunt, nor the Post Modernists, attempt to inform or overwhelm via the grand scale. The elements of form are both literally and figuratively within reach.

Bryan Hunt is the only artist of his generation to knit the fanciful elements of twentieth century *tromp l'oeil,* the contradictions of Post Modernist spaces, and the surfaces and techniques of traditional sculpture (and rendering). From this vantage point, his work is rightfully placed in the forefront of creative invention. With the figurative voids, as Carter Ratcliff noted, "Hunt seems to be on the verge of teaching the elements of architecture to take on a human presence."[5]

Constance W. Glenn

Notes

[1] The vase/face, later adapted by Jasper Johns in ***Cups 4 Picasso,*** *is regarded as the creation of Danish psychologist Edgar Rubin.*

[2] Martin Friedman and Graham W. J. Beal, ***George Segal: Sculptures*** *(Minneapolis: Walker Art Center, 1978), p. 72.*

[3] Constance W. Glenn, ***George Segal: Pastels 1957-1965*** *(Long Beach: California State University, 1977), p. 10.*

[4] Robert Jensen and Patricia Conway, ***Ornamentalism,*** *(New York: Clarkson N. Potter, Inc., 1982), pp. 20-21. The references are to Post-Modern architecture, but are applied here to the work of Bryan Hunt.*

[5] Carter Ratcliff, ***Bryan Hunt*** *(New York and Los Angeles: Blum Helman Gallery and Margo Leavin Gallery, 1983), np.*

BRYAN HUNT
Drawing

An Immediate and Autonomous Act

"Le dessin, c'est l'ecriture de l'âme, et c'est vraiment in lui que réside toute la personnalité du sculpteur." [1]

— *Raymond Martin*

Drawing has always been closely associated with sculpting. A study of the drawings done by a sculptor affords the viewer an insight into the essence of the artist's personality. Sculptor Bryan Hunt declares, "I love to draw — it is the most direct experience in terms of making art . . . it is that blank space . . . anytime you confront yourself with a blank page you attach yourself to a continuum of people doing that . . . it has the most dexterity, it's immediate and expressive." [2] Almost all sculptors draw. They do so for a variety of reasons, in a variety of styles, and they use a variety of media. They share the need to express their feelings through the immediacy of the discipline because, as David Smith stated, "Drawing remains the life force of the artist. This is especially true for the sculptor who works in media slow to take realization and where the original creative impulse must be maintained during labor."[3] Although Hunt's sculptures are as individual as his drawing style, his reasons for drawing and the goals or purposes of the drawings can be compared generally and specifically with those of other sculptors throughout the ages.

A drawing has been defined as an image obtained by marking on a surface — a delineation — the basis of pictorial experience sometimes accompanied with effects of light and dark.[4] This pedantic explanation, however, does not include the adjectives that are often associated with drawings — delightful, intimate, spontaneous, direct — that give them their significant connotations. The first inspirations, thoughts and impressions of the artist are revealed in his drawings. They will, most likely, define the end result. Some drawings, as compared with paintings, are the art of omission.[5] These are simpler and more abstract but, therefore, can be more sophisticated with their limited line, modeling and color that beg the viewer to fill in the necessary detail. Others can be more complete, complex or highly refined.

Most drawings were not saved or collected prior to the middle of the fourteenth century. The earliest collectors were students of well-known masters who, realizing their worth, would appropriate the works when the master died. Vasari and Dürer collected drawings as part of their research and investigation.[6] By the middle of the fifteenth century drawings became ends in themselves and were collected as such.[7] As the discipline of drawing became ever more important, the ruling houses of Europe started to amass important collections. It was not until the eighteenth century, however, that a few scholars and art dealers who appreciated the value of drawings began to purchase them.[8] While drawing, for some painters, became less important with the use of color and the breakdown of form in the late nineteenth and early twentieth centuries, drawing as an autonomous art form gradually developed and became equal to art forms in other media.[9]

Although Bryan Hunt's drawings can stand alone, they are related to his sculpture in the similarity of their concepts. The drawings enhance the artist's and the viewer's appreciation, enjoyment and awareness of the sculpture. Hunt's drawings progress through their own variations and can sometimes be years in advance of their sculptural counterparts. He explains, "I did a drawing two years ago that I kept in my studio. I looked over at it one day and realized I had just recently made it into a sculpture . . . it was that far advanced."[10] At times he does use drawing to resolve sculptural problems. He experiments, trying to see his drawings in a three-dimensional way. But, for the most part, they serve as drawings in and of themselves.[11] Many could never exist as sculpture; they, therefore, have a flexibility that sculpture does not have.[12] On a long wall in his studio Hunt displays and studies his recent drawings. "I don't make a lot of drawings but when I do make them they happen fairly fast. With that kind of line, with the idea of drawing a line as an expression, you can't hold back and premeditate. You've got to follow — go from 'A' to 'B' and back."[13]

Hunt's philosophy of art and style of drawing are close to those of the contemporary artists who have been aligned with the New Image or New Figuration groups.[14] They are concerned with isolating and simplifying representational forms for expressionistic purposes.[15] Realism itself is peripheral to the chief goal of those artists who use the image as an inherited format or an interpretive device for their own personal intentions.[16] It is a universal imagery, abstract, yet concrete and familiar (No. 41). It is Hunt's interest in decontextualizing these images that is akin to the New Image painters.

During his travels Hunt has sketched everything from the Classical architecture and the sculpture of ancient Greece to the works of Michelangelo. Natural phenomena have also inspired him. "Nature in landscape becomes the figure," he says. "Lakes and quarries are reclining, waterfalls are the opposite."[17] When drawing a landscape he begins with references to specific images. He will start with the top of a lake as seen on a two-dimensional plane and then fantasize about the bottom as it is dictated by the surface (No. 23). In this way his drawings function between the representational and the abstract, thus becoming universal.[18] In other drawings, first read as abstract forms, the viewer, upon contemplation, can isolate references to Classical Grecian urns or figures, the former purportedly based upon the female form (No. 30).[19] Hunt uses water, the most abstract of all images, and what he calls the "ultimate receiver," to interpret these forms.[20] Like drapery on a figure, his water falls from a point of anchorage to a point of impact, but it is removed from all surrounding elements of the land that gives it form.

To best capture the image and feeling that he wants to project, Hunt uses a good grade of paper that will hold up when he paints on it with linseed oil. The oil acts as a coloring agent as it ripens into an ivory hue in about a month. The area painted with the oil also acts as a path for graphite and, with the use of turpentine, breaks this substance down, making the line more fluid so that it can "happen without resistance . . . My drawings are all about line," Hunt notes. "I love to draw a line. I love the idea that you can make a variation on a line that has an emotion itself, or that you can put lines together and this juxtaposition creates another tone."[21] Some of his lines are delicate and some are smudged and broken where they do not precisely follow the oiled area (No. 24). His aquaintance with Minimal Art once prompted him to use horizontal and vertical lines and avoid diagonals. "But," he states, "as soon as I got into the landscape, natural diagonals became apparent and not just an arbitrary decision."[22] His choice of which area to intensify or which to leave white, in what starts essentially as a line drawing, is what distinguishes his conceptualizations. "If I just want to make a line, I'll make that gesture. If I see what I want to achieve is that inner relationship between the figure and the landscape, or the falls as the figure, or the negative shape of the falls as the figure . . . the lines are the signals on the paper that you can read as the form. Somehow, all of a sudden, you perceive that the line is both a figurative line and exists in the landscape at the same time (No. 38)."[23] Often he expands the lines until they fill the whole page. Sometimes there is very little white space remaining, and at other times the white space predominates, becoming the figure itself. This interplay of positive and negative space yields an image that is formed by the landscape even though the landscape itself is not apparent. He relies on the white of the paper in combination with jagged black lines to create a sense of the velocity and liveliness of the freely falling water that gives the figure its animation. The dense profusion of black marks creates a turbulent power. The graphite strokes are longer and more fluid where the water falls straight and are short and choppy where it comes into contact with the base (No. 11).

Hunt's drawings are part of the long history of drawings done by sculptors. Many of the artists in this tradition have believed in Henry Moore's credo, "Good vision in drawing will come out in the sculpture."[24] A few, like Cellini and Houdon, preferred modeling first, while others, such as Greenough, drew mainly for their patrons' benefit.[25] The first reference to a sculptor's use of drawing appears in the eleventh century in *The Various Acts* by the German monk Theophilus. He instructed his pupils to spread chalk over the bone they were to carve, then draw figures with lead, and score the

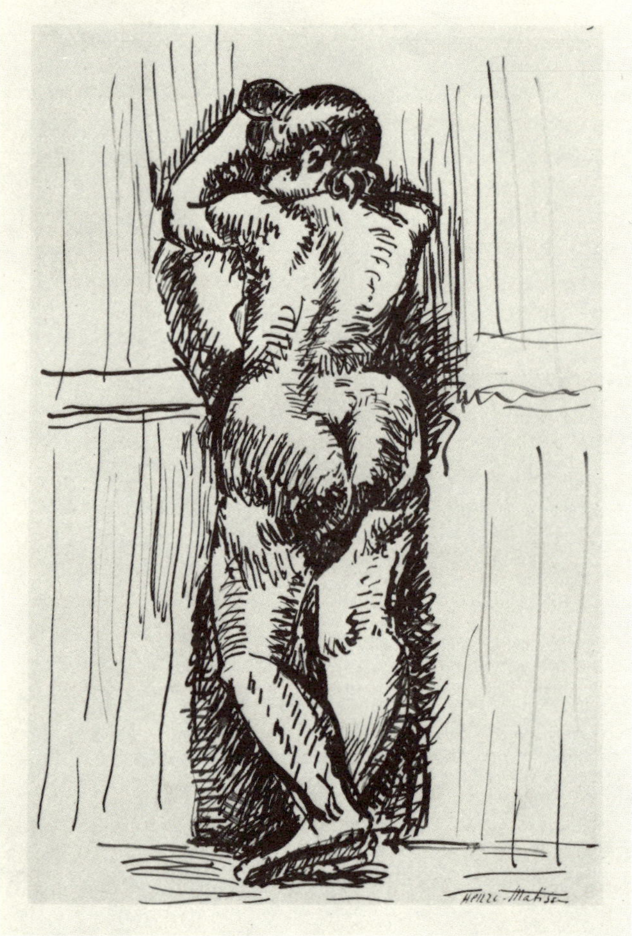

Figure 5. *Henri Matisse,* ***Study of a Model's Back,*** *1910, pen, brown ink; 11⅜ x 7⅝. Courtesy of The National Gallery of Canada, Ottawa.*

outlines with a sharp tracer.[26] The earliest known sculptor's drawing, circa 1350 to 1360, represents a design for a chancel for the Cathedral at Orvieto.[27] Over the centuries drawings by sculptors have become increasingly more important, and since the 1930s many sculptors have drawn and painted autonomously.[28]

The question arises as to whether or not sculptors draw differently than painters. Many sculptors' drawings appear to lack the energy or vigor of painters' drawings because they stress contour, volume and mass instead of the detailed rendering of images. Some contend that drawing an image too completely lessens their ultimate desire to reproduce the work in a three-dimensional form.

Sculptors' drawings, which ultimately have the capacity to bridge the gap between two-and three-dimensional expression, fall into several categories. Some are actually schematic designs or working drawings that will often have specifications concerning contour, detail, dimension or even process. They can manifest several different views. Other drawings vary from autonomous creations to variations on a theme such as Brancusi's progressions from realist to abstract form. Modigliani would play with a theme for years, never satisfied that all the possibilities were exhausted, just as Hunt has been involved with the variations on the waterfall.

Hunt's forms appear chiselled or even chopped in places, recalling some of Matisse's earlier drawings that reveal an expressionist urgency with intense sharp jabs and coarse pen marks creating a dynamic surface with tension and conflict. When Matisse approached drawing with sculpture in mind, he changed his fluid decorative line to short choppy strokes, giving the feeling of actual sculpture techniques (fig. 5).[29]

When Hunt is drawing he can become carried away with the activity, making one work after another in succession. Sometimes his drawings are set aside only to be brought out later and referred to for further study. The drawings of Henry Moore and Kenneth Armitage often predict what will later become a sculpture.[30] Other drawings, however, like some of those of Bernini and Hunt, are complete fantasies that were never intended to be translated to stone or bronze. Although Bernini would often return to his drawings, he set them aside when he started sculpting, saying, "I don't want to copy from myself but to create an original work."[31] On a more contemporary level, David Smith stated, " . . . my work comes from drawings. Not specifically. If I know all about it in drawing, then I don't have to use a drawing to make a sculpture . . . "[32]

In referring to his involvement with paper, oil and graphite, Bryan Hunt concludes, "Drawing has always functioned for me, whether its intention is to be a sculpture or just a drawing. It is an activity that is fulfilling. Sometimes it is exactly what the sculpture is or will be . . . and sometimes it's just working through a day."[33] No matter what his intent, his drawings are works of art that follow in a long tradition of drawings by sculptors — intimate works regarded as the artists' most personal expressions.

Shirley Pinard

Notes

[1] *Raymond Martin, quoted in W. J. Strachan,* ***Towards Sculpture*** *(Boulder, Colorado: Westview Press, 1976), p. 15; "Drawing is the writing of the soul, and the entire personality of the sculptor truly resides there."*

[2] *Bryan Hunt Interview, California State University Long Beach, April 25, 1983.*

[3] *W.J. Strachan,* ***Towards Sculpture*** *(Boulder, Colorado: Westview Press, 1976), p. 140.*

[4] *Daniel M. Mendelowitz,* ***Drawing*** *(New York: Holt, Rinehart and Winston, Inc., 1967), p. 8.*

[5] ***Great Drawings of the Masters,*** *ed. J. E. Schuler and Dr. Rolf Hansler (New York: G. P. Putnam's Sons, 1963), p. 24.*

[6] *Schuler, p. 10.*

[7] *Schuler, p. 20.*

[8] *Schuler, pp. 14-16.*

[9] *Heribert Hutter,* ***Drawing, History and Technique*** *(New York: McGraw-Hill Book Company, 1966), p. 7.*

[10] *Bryan Hunt Interview, California State University Long Beach, February 9, 1983.*

[11] *Robin White, "Bryan Hunt,"* ***View*** *(April 1980): 21.*

[12] *Hunt, February 9, 1983.*

[13] *White, p. 21.*

[14] *White, p. 15.*

[15] *Dupuy Warrick Reed, "Bryan Hunt,"* ***Flash Art*** *104 (October/November 1981): 49.*

[16] *Amy Benenson, "Aspects of Abstract Representation," in* ***Hunt, Jenney, Lane, Rothenberg, Shapiro,*** *edited by Peter Morrin (Poughkeepsie, New York: Vassar College Art Gallery, 1978), np.*

[17] *Bryan Hunt, quoted in Constance Glenn, "Artist's Dialogue,"* ***Architectural Digest*** *68 (March 1983): 72.*

[18] *White, p. 4.*

[19] *Strachan,* ***Towards Sculpture,*** *p. 81; "Antoine Bourdelle, when not indulging in academic stylization, reveals some of the best qualities we associate with Antiquity. The shape of the Grecian urn is said to have been inspired by the female torso; hence the title of his bronze,* ***The Urn.****"*

[20] *Reed, p. 49.*

[21] *White, p. 21*

[22] *Reed, p. 49.*

[23] *Hunt, February 9, 1983.*

[24] *Henry Moore, quoted in Strachan,* ***Towards Sculpture,*** *p. 140.*

[25] *Colin Eisler,* ***Sculptors' Drawings Over Six Centuries 1400-1950*** *(New York: Agrinde Publications Ltd., 1981), np.*

[26] *Eisler, np.*

[27] *Hutter, p. 82.*

[28] *Deborah C. Phillips, "Where Painting and Sculpture Meet,"* ***ARTnews*** *80 (June 1980): 248.*

[29] *Elizabeth Ann Brown, "Sculptors' Drawings,"* ***Arts Magazine*** *55 (June 1981): 22.*

[30] *W. J. Strachan, "The Sculptor and His Drawings,"* ***Connoisseur*** *186 (July 1974): 186.*

[31] *Bernini, quoted in Eisler, np.*

[32] *Smith, quoted in Eisler, np.*

[33] *Hunt, April 25, 1983.*

BRYAN HUNT
Between Above and Below

The Coexistance of Minimal Art and Reality

" . . . the difference between the present and the past is that the conscious present is an awareness of the past in a way and to an extent which the past's awareness of itself cannot show."

— T.S. Eliot

Some artists react. They attempt to divest themselves of the rules, conventions and guidelines of those who came before. They fancy themselves revolutionary. They are, typically, extremists, dogmatic in their approach to art. Other artists assimilate. Rather than try to wholly discard the past, they search for the positive lessons inherent in what has been and use these as foundations and/or springboards for their own personal investigations. Their manner of working is often slow, their progress evolutionary. Some say such tendencies (revolutionary versus evolutionary) characterize entire periods in history and that these tendencies alternate in cyclical patterns. While such a generalization is always dangerous, one can, nevertheless, often discern such a pattern. The period of the late sixties/early seventies saw the emergence of art movements (Minimalism, Conceptualism, Performance and Earth art) which demonstrated very radical perceptions regarding the nature of art. In the case of Minimalism, perhaps the most pervasive of these tendencies, there was an air of impersonality and finality in its statement. There seemed little more the following generation of artists could do to further Minimalist ideals. Instead, what one finds is that artists today are re-examining more subjective aspects of art such as imagery, figuration, symbolism and self-expression, but, it must be added, with the additional insight that is the legacy of the late sixties' radicalism.

Bryan Hunt is an excellent example of the latter assimilatory tendency. If the titling of a work of art may be said to be the first act in a continuum of interpretation, then perhaps the most prophetic title that Bryan Hunt has ever given to one of his own works is *Kan,* from the *I Ching,* meaning "between above and below."[1] That title seems a fitting analogy for the whole of Hunt's work, which, in combining ideologies of the recent past with aspects of his personal vision, is an art that embraces elements which are, by nature, diametrically opposed. The appeal of his work is in the dynamic interaction of such contradictory aspects and their subsequent harmonization as the artist finds that elusive point of balance "between" them.

"For me the best thing was to hit the line, that line of coexistence — coexistence between Minimal art and reality . . . "[2]

— Bryan Hunt

At the beginning of this century, for the first time in the history of Western art, paintings and sculpture were created which were essentially devoid of representational imagery. Wassily Kandinsky, among the first to create non-objective paintings, expressed a concern for the content of these new expressions. Without recognizable subject matter, he feared art would be dismissed as decorative, so he insisted on a spiritual content for his work.[3] By the late sixties, one art form had developed that completely disposed of extraneous content: Minimalism. This exclusivity meant the elimination of any referential meanings, of personal feelings and associations, in order to produce, "A response that is exclusively aesthetic."[4] It was an art about itself or, as Frank Stella explained it, "Only what can be seen there is there."[5] In the avoidance of representational and expressionist forms, and the ambiguous meanings associated with them, an art of absolute clarity was to develop.

A knowledge of this Minimalist reasoning is one of the conditions helpful in understanding Hunt's work, for he says, "I take Minimal ideas very seriously."[6] This is evident in his work. His waterfall sculptures do have a sense of being intrinsically "whole," a value prescribed by Donald Judd in his essay, *Specific Objects.* Perhaps this is felt most forcefully by the viewer who has no preconceptions, no prior knowledge of Hunt's work, and therefore has an unschooled, purely aesthetic response. In such an instance, what is perceived in a piece such as *First Fall II,* 1978 (fig. 6) is a strong unity of sculptural mass com-

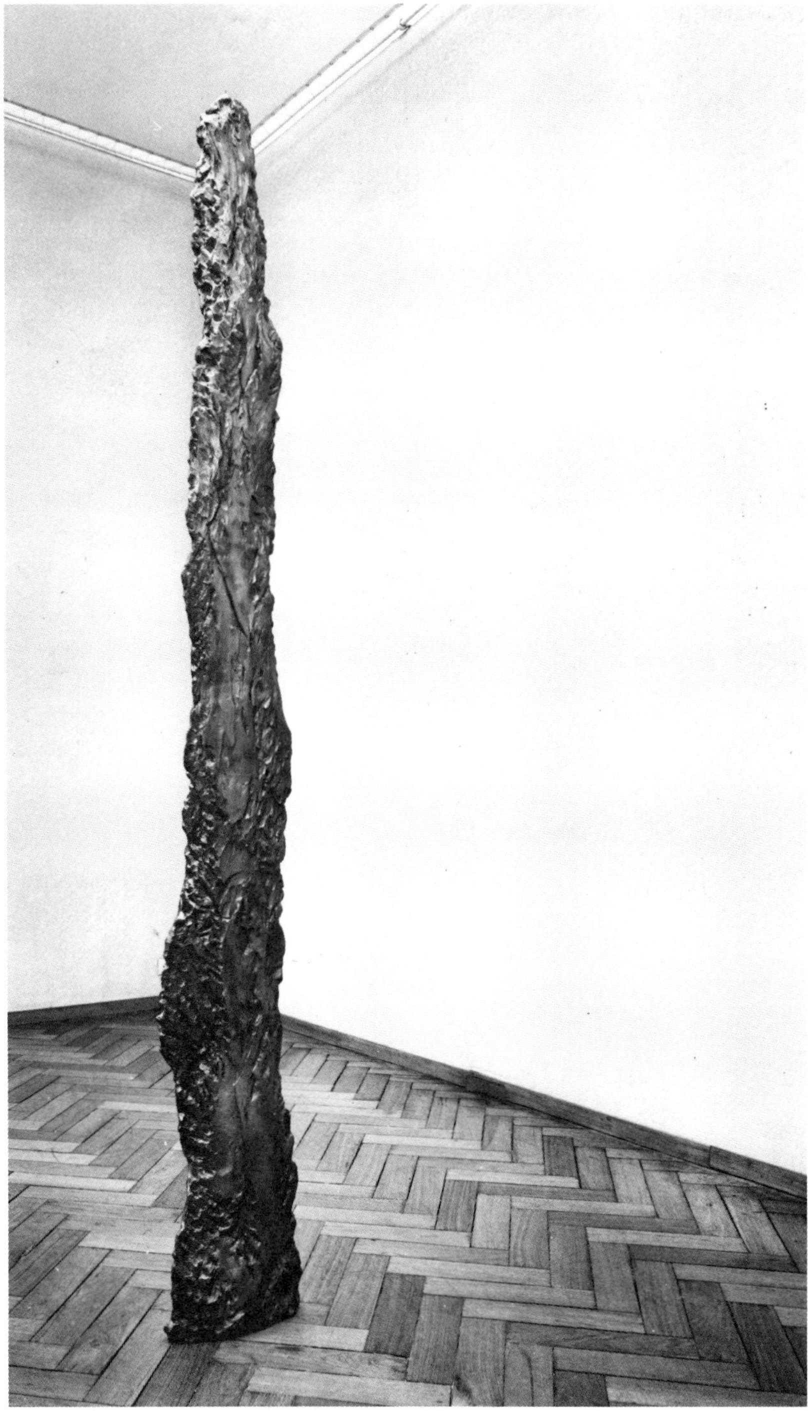

Figure 6. *Bryan Hunt,* ***First Fall II,*** *1978, bronze. Photograph courtesy of Blum Helman.*

parable to that found in a Robert Morris slab or John McCracken plank. Nothing, not the "shape, image, color or surface is partial or scattered."[7] The sculpture maintains what Hunt calls Minimal art's "amazing presence." He sees no need to " . . . fill anything in," that is, to make external allusions. But he breaks from the Minimalists when he says " . . . you *can* fill anything in of course, as you do with any art."[8]

Hunt is one of the many artists (often grouped together as the "New Image" artists for want of a movement) who began to question the validity of Minimalism and its alleged fusion of form and content. Its reductivist logic appeared to many to be sterile, stifling creativity. Furthermore, the Minimalist "object presence" could easily be construed to have the cabalistic spiritual meaning espoused by Kandinsky a half century earlier. Ultimately, the fact remains that these objects are human creations and their function is humanly intended.[9] To explain this function, "no art has ever been more dependent on words than that pledged to silent materiality."[10] Recognition of these problems undermines the Minimalist notion of the self-sufficient art object.

Hunt recognizes the limitations of the Minimalist primary form. "It's such a refinement of form that if you expand on it, or if you put a surface on it, or if you articulate it to an image or to an icon, or to something that translates midway into that, then to me that's going one step beyond it. You can't refine the square."[11] Hunt overcomes Minimalism's restrictive boundaries by simply allowing, both for himself and the viewer, a great liberty in interpretation.

"The vehicle I can use is the experience of a very contemporary idea of presence on the planet."[12] This statement implies that Hunt feels free to incorporate any experiential occurence into a work of art. For example, one of the main themes in his work is the waterfall, a theme that began as a personal response to an external natural phenomenon, a response the Minimalists would never have allowed. But, unlike pre-modern representation, his is not a literal translation of visual reality. Rather, he uses a phenomenal fact of nature, the waterfall, as an "interpretive device," or a starting point from which he elaborates as he translates it through successive stages of conceptual, sculptural and perceptual reality. "The idea is not to have the experience of reality, but to have the experience of a shift in scale from reality to object as sculpture."[13] For Hunt, however, the arrival at the final stage of the translative process, the sculpture, does not mean that the preceding stages need to be eliminated.

Conceptual ideas remain a very important aspect of his work, perhaps creating a tenuous affinity with the Conceptual artists of the late sixties/early seventies who stressed art as idea to the exclusion of any object at all (another example of the period's radicalism). More probably, it is an identification with the artists who made earth works such as Robert Smithson, Walter De Maria and Michael Heizer. These artists translated their conceptual ideas into monumental realities, drawing mile long lines in the desert or displacing 240,000 tons of earth at the rim of a canyon. But it has been pointed out that, ". . . Earth art is both conceptual and perceptual. That is it is perceptual for the person doing it or seeing it, but for the rest of us it can only exist in the mind."[14] Typically, these works are located in remote areas, isolated from the everyday world. Hunt works with similarly monumental concepts but, in a more practical vein, manages to clothe them in more compact sculptural forms. The conceptual aspect of his work is thus in strange diametric opposition to the sculptural aspect: a conceptually monumental phenomenon, the waterfall, exists together with a sculpturally intimate form; the phenomenally fluid and dynamic (again, the waterfall in nature) is conceived of as frozen in permanent stasis. Neither component of his methodology (perceptual or conceptual) entirely supercedes the other, rather it is, as he says, the "shift" that is important, the translation that is the creative act.

This flexibility in expressive definition is one of Hunt's great attributes and he extends the same freedom to the viewer. Actually, his attitude toward the spectator is merely realistic. A viewer will bring to a work of art his own perceptions, associations and feelings regardless of the artist's intentions. It has often been said that Hunt's work has sexually symbolic undertones. Both his waterfalls and airships have a certain phallic quality. The Minimalists would have regarded this associative reference as needless interference. Carl Andre, for example, denied emphatically that his work had any implicit sexual meaning, even though, in putting Brancusi's *Endless Column* on the ground, he implied inheritance of the original work's phallic symbolism.[15] Hunt, on the other hand, does not deny the metaphoric or symbolic nature of his art. "I think they're symbolic mainly because they manifest unconscious mechanisms (of male and female energy)."[16]

Bryan Hunt is an artist with a profound understanding of the past and his own relationship to it. Not only does he understand his tradition, he utilizes it and, together with aspects of the world in which he lives and his own personality, he creates an art of infinite possibilities, one that combines diverse realities in such a way as to allow seemingly antithetical situations to resolve into harmonious existence. That is one of the great powers of art.

"I'm like that in a lot of things. It's a distinct polarization, but it also kind of fits — like a mobius strip. It fits where the extremes meet." [17]

— Bryan Hunt

Jeffery Matsuno

Notes

[1] *Melinda Wortz, "Hieroglyphic Umbrellas,"* ***ARTnews,*** *May 1980, p. 141.*

[2] *Robin White, "Interview,"* ***View*** *(Oakland, California: Crown Point Press), April 1980, p. 6.*

[3] *Rose Carol Washton-Long, "Kandinsky and Abstraction," in Patricia Kaplan and Susan Manso (eds.)* ***Major European Art Movements*** *(New York: E.P. Dutton, 1977), p. 277.*

[4] *Harold Rosenberg, "Defining Art," reprinted from* ***The New Yorker,*** *February 25, 1967 in Gregory Battock (ed.),* ***Minimal Art: A Critical Anthology*** *(New York: E.P. Dutton, 1968), p. 303.*

[5] *Ellen H. Johnson,* ***Modern Art and The Object*** *(New York: Harper & Row Publishers, 1976), p. 16.*

[6] *White, p. 6.*

[7] *Donald Judd, "Specific Objects," in* ***Contemporary Sculpture, Arts Yearbook 8*** *(New York: The Art Digest, Inc., 1965), p. 78.*

[8] *White, p. 7.*

[9] *Peter Morrin, "Introduction,"* ***Hunt, Jenney, Lane, Rothenberg, Shapiro*** *(Poughkeepsie, New York: Vassar College Art Gallery, 1978), np.*

[10] *Rosenberg, p. 304.*

[11] *White, p. 6.*

[12] *Ibid., p. 8.*

[13] *Ibid., p. 4.*

[14] *Johnson, p. 41.*

[15] *David Bourdon, "The Razed Sites of Carl Andre," in Gregory Battock (ed.)* ***Minimal Art: A Critical Anthology*** *(New York: E.P. Dutton, 1968), p. 104.*

[16] *White, p. 14.*

[17] *Ibid., p. 8.*

BRYAN HUNT
The Landscape

Why do people love landscape? Hills and gardens restore our nature, so we should visit them often. Springs and rocks are good for carefree rambling, so we delight in them. In landscapes we become fishermen, woodcutters, and hermits — with monkeys, cranes, and birds as our frequent companions.[1]

— Kuo Hsi
(Active around 1050-90), painter and theorist.

For centuries man has been involved in creating art which has had some direct link with nature. This link has taken countless shapes: from realistic depictions, to abstracted forms, to artists working directly on the surface of the earth. In the last decade, Bryan Hunt, through the utilization of primary shapes and forms of the natural landscape, has established his own unique position in this realm.

Hunt's drawings are not meant to be a mimesis of reality. Commenting on his working techniques, he says: "We speak privately, I add, I subtract, I wait, I pace. We're alone and uncertain. Then a line of a thousand visions holds true and it releases into space . . . Those ghostly images in the mountains could translate into a line drawing of falls. But it doesn't have to be a fall, it can just be that mysterious shape, a shadow in the mountain . . . The waterfalls are developing their own metamorphosis; they are going somewhere else. If you have a line, and you also have my language somehow introduced to you, say through my past work, and if you have 'waterfall' in the back of your mind and you are taken to another spot, then that's where I would be going."[2]

C. Michelle Betty

Notes

*[1] Kuo Hsi, quoted in Wen Fong, **Summer Mountains** (New York: The Metropolitan Museum of Modern Art, 1975), p. 1.*

*[2] Bryan Hunt is quoted in: Robin White, "Interview with Bryan Hunt," **View** (Oakland, California: Crown Point Press) April, 1980, p. 22, p. 18; and from Bryan Hunt Interview, California State University, Long Beach, April 25, 1983.*

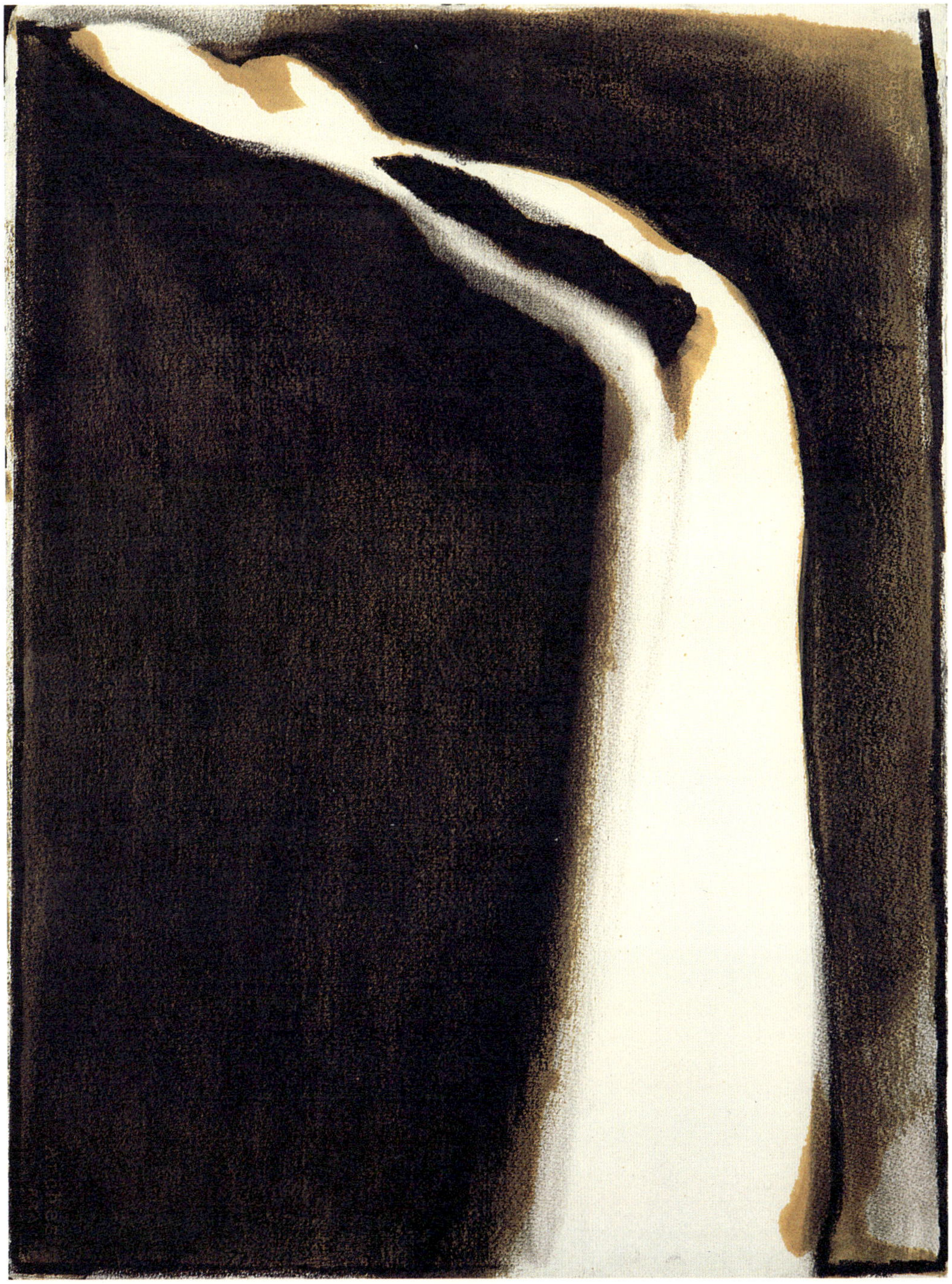

No. 6
Myst, *1977*
graphite and linseed oil
on Arches paper
30¼ x 22½"

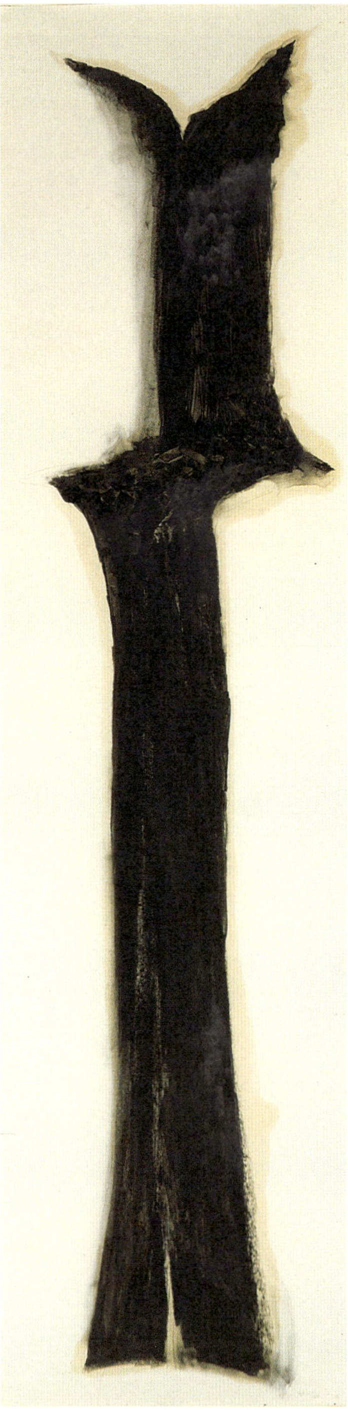

No. 11
***Black Falls IX,** 1978*
graphite and linseed oil on paper
84¾ x 21¼"

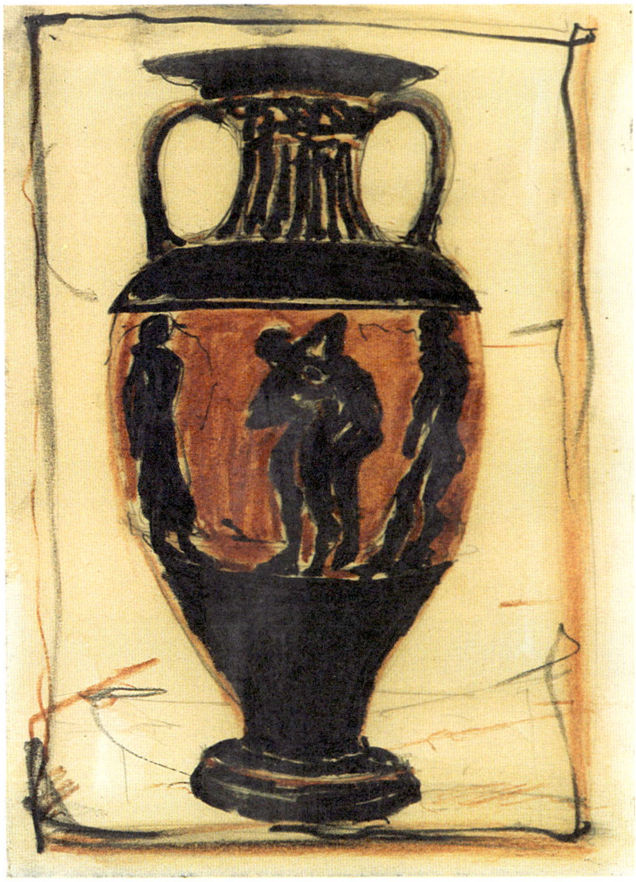

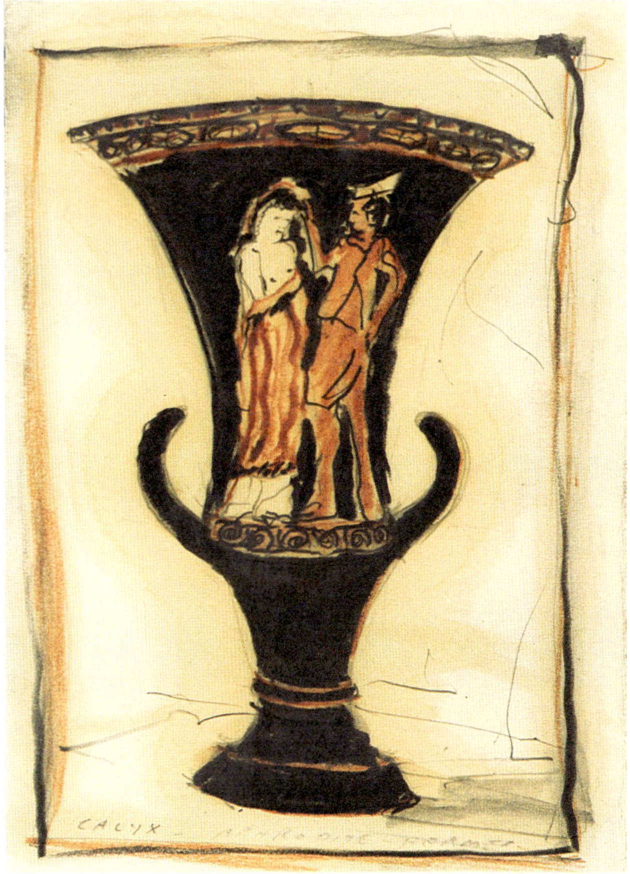

No. 40
***Grecian Study,** 1982 (left)*
graphite, linseed oil and conte crayon on paper
8¾ x 6⅜"

No. 35
***Calyx-Aphrodite-Hermes,** 1982 (right)*
graphite, linseed oil and conte crayon on paper
8¾ x 6⅜"

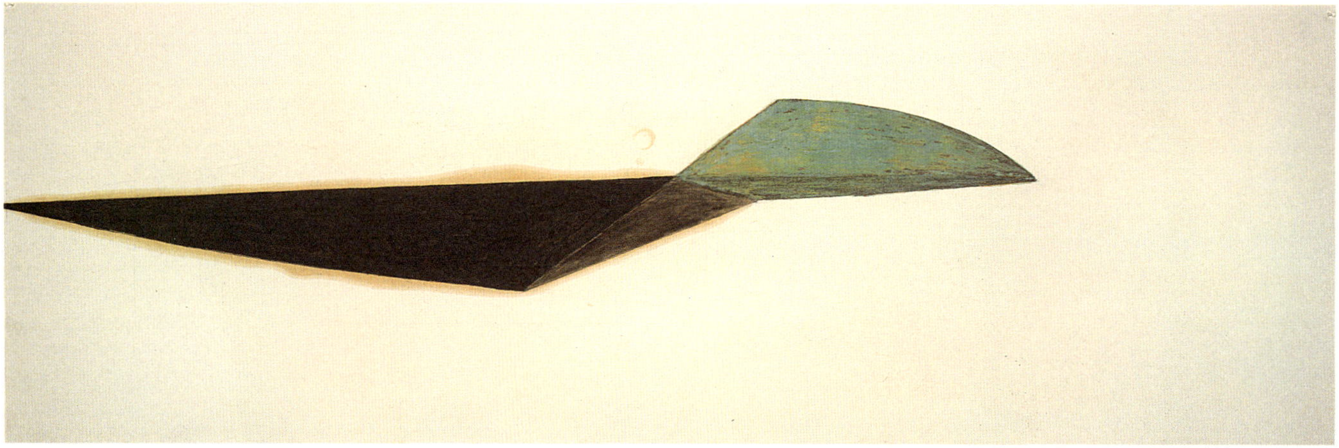

No. 31
Limn Drawing, *1981*
graphite, linseed oil and copper leaf on paper
28 x 84"

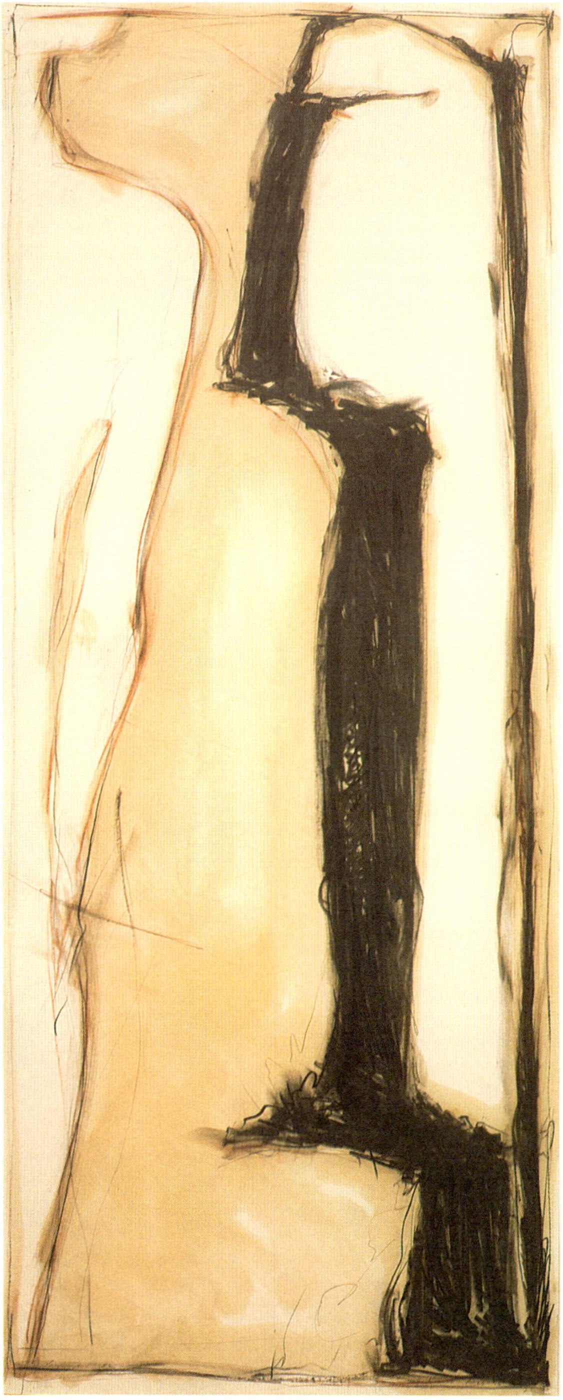

No. 38
Converse Passage, *1982*
graphite, linseed oil and conte crayon on paper
84½ x 34⅛"

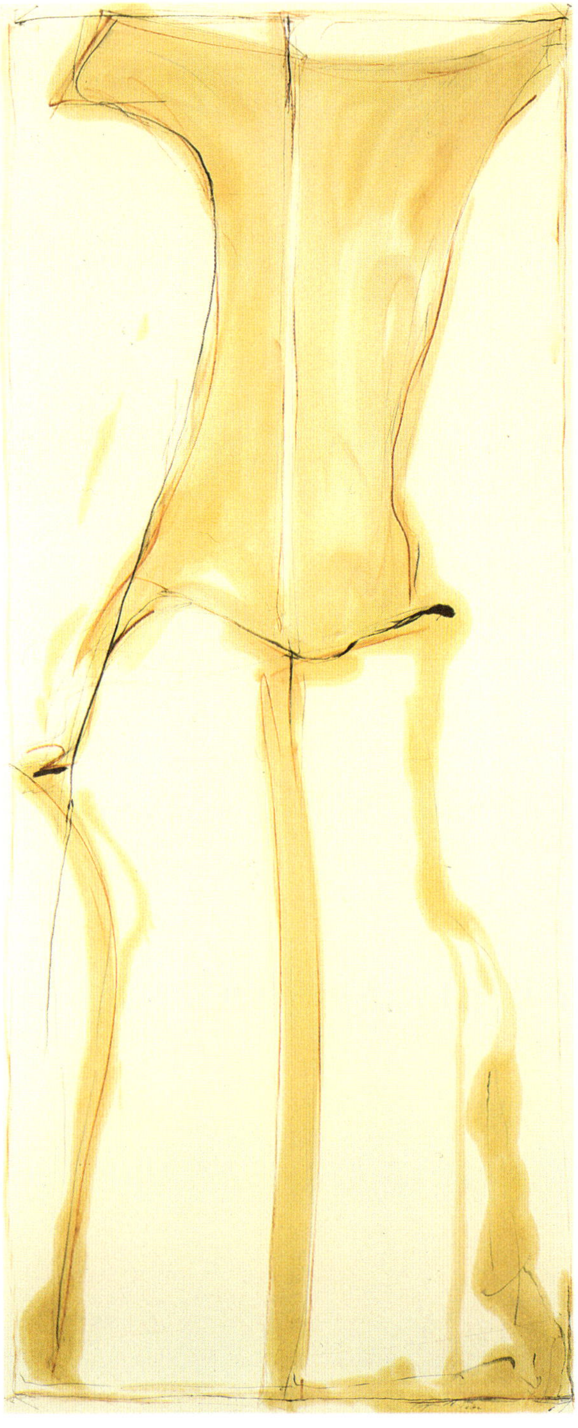

No. 41
***Proserpine,** 1982*
graphite, conte crayon and linseed oil on paper
85 x 35 "

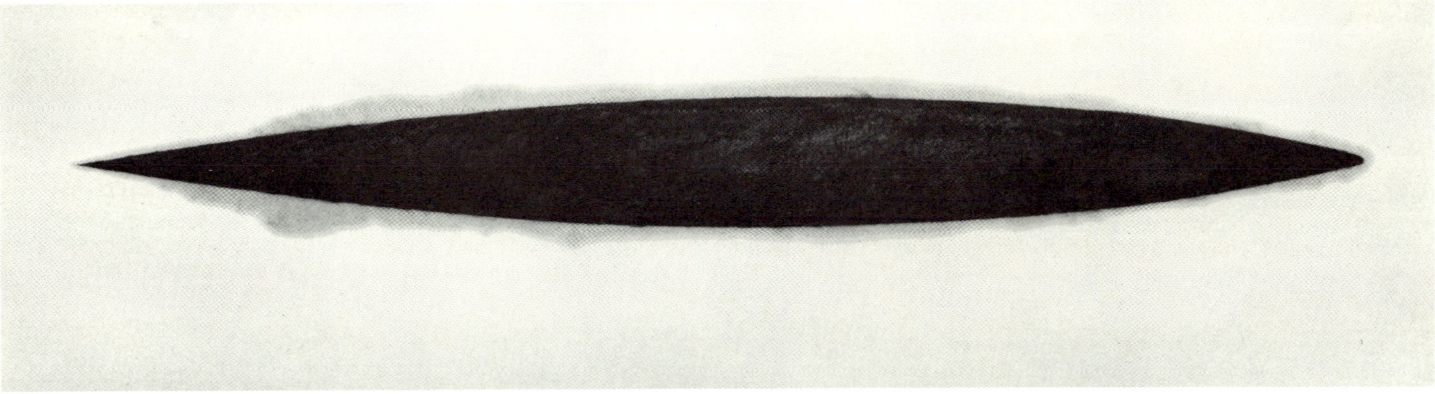

No. 3
Ship Shape, *1974*
graphite and linseed oil on paper
24 x 87½"

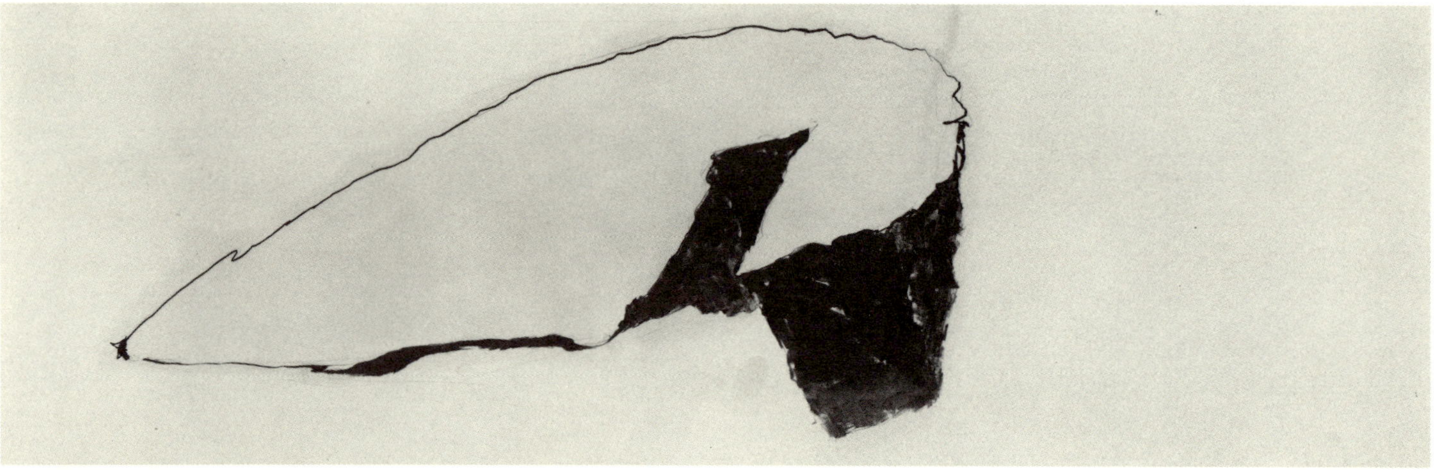

No. 23
Cubit Quarry, *1980*
graphite and linseed oil on paper
24 x 71¾"

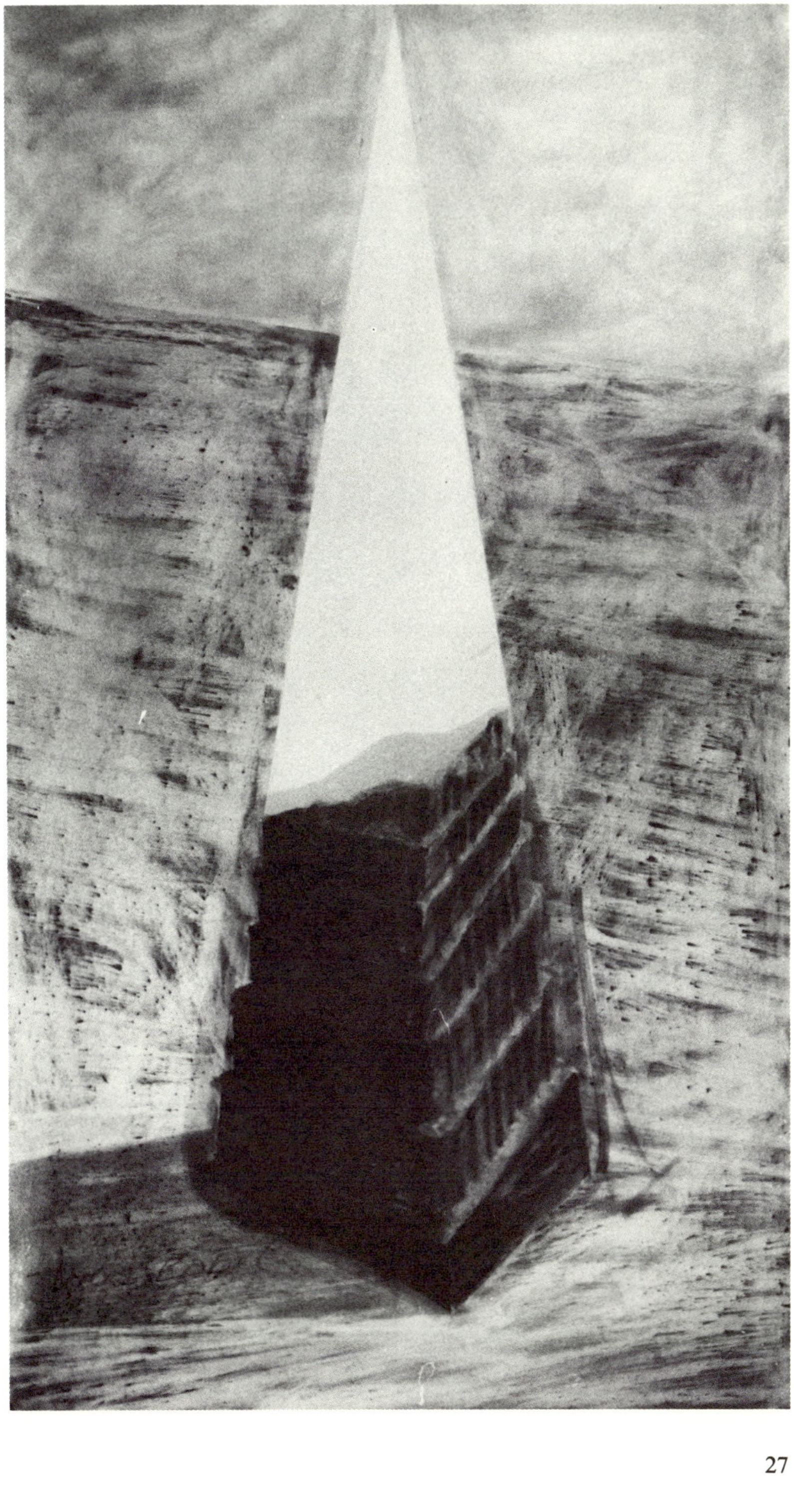

No. 5
Tower of Babel I, *1975 (Pyramidal),*
graphite and linseed oil on Arches paper
46½ x 29"

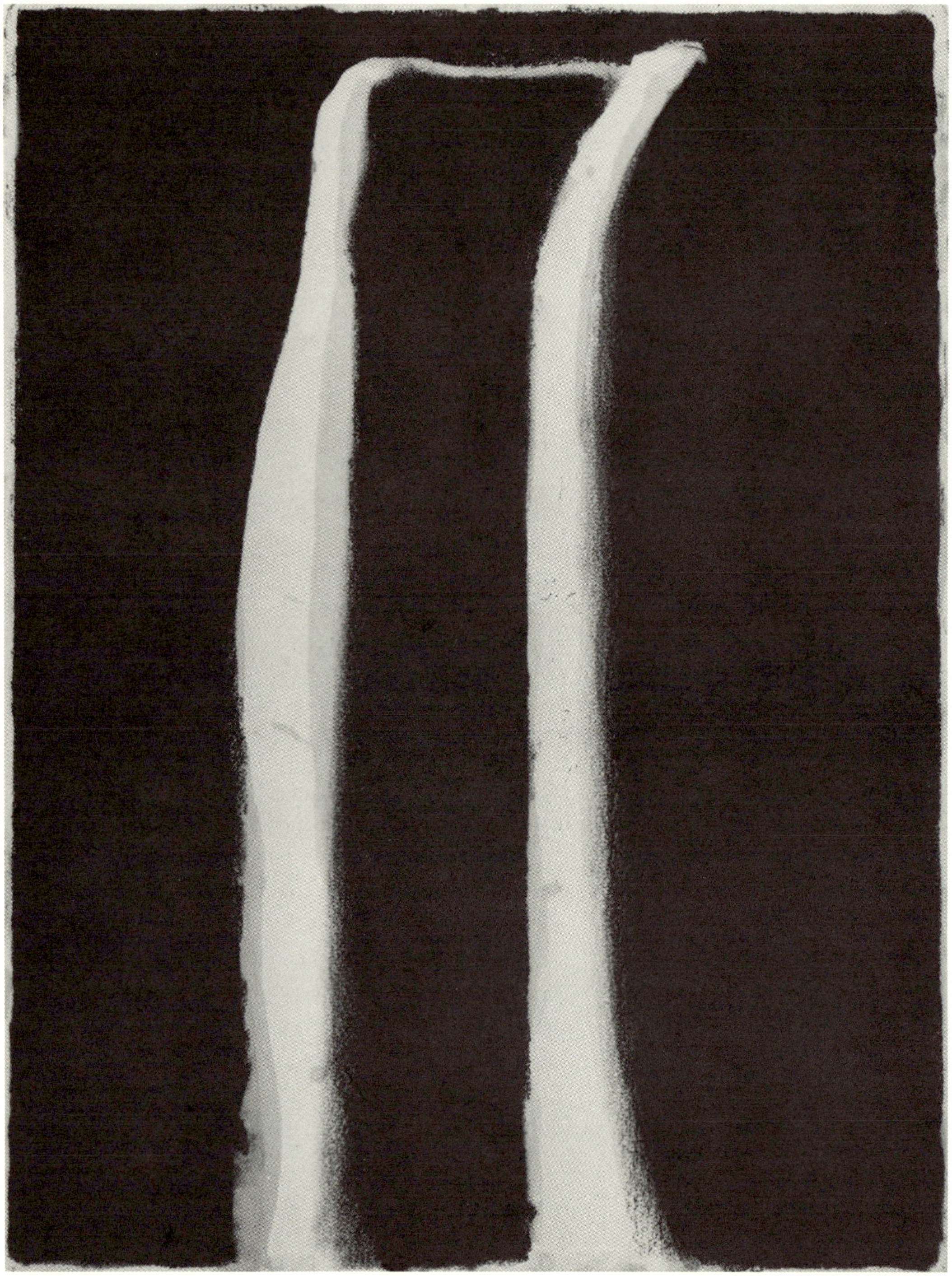

No. 8
Twin Falls, *1977*
graphite and linseed oil
on Arches paper
30¼ x 22½"

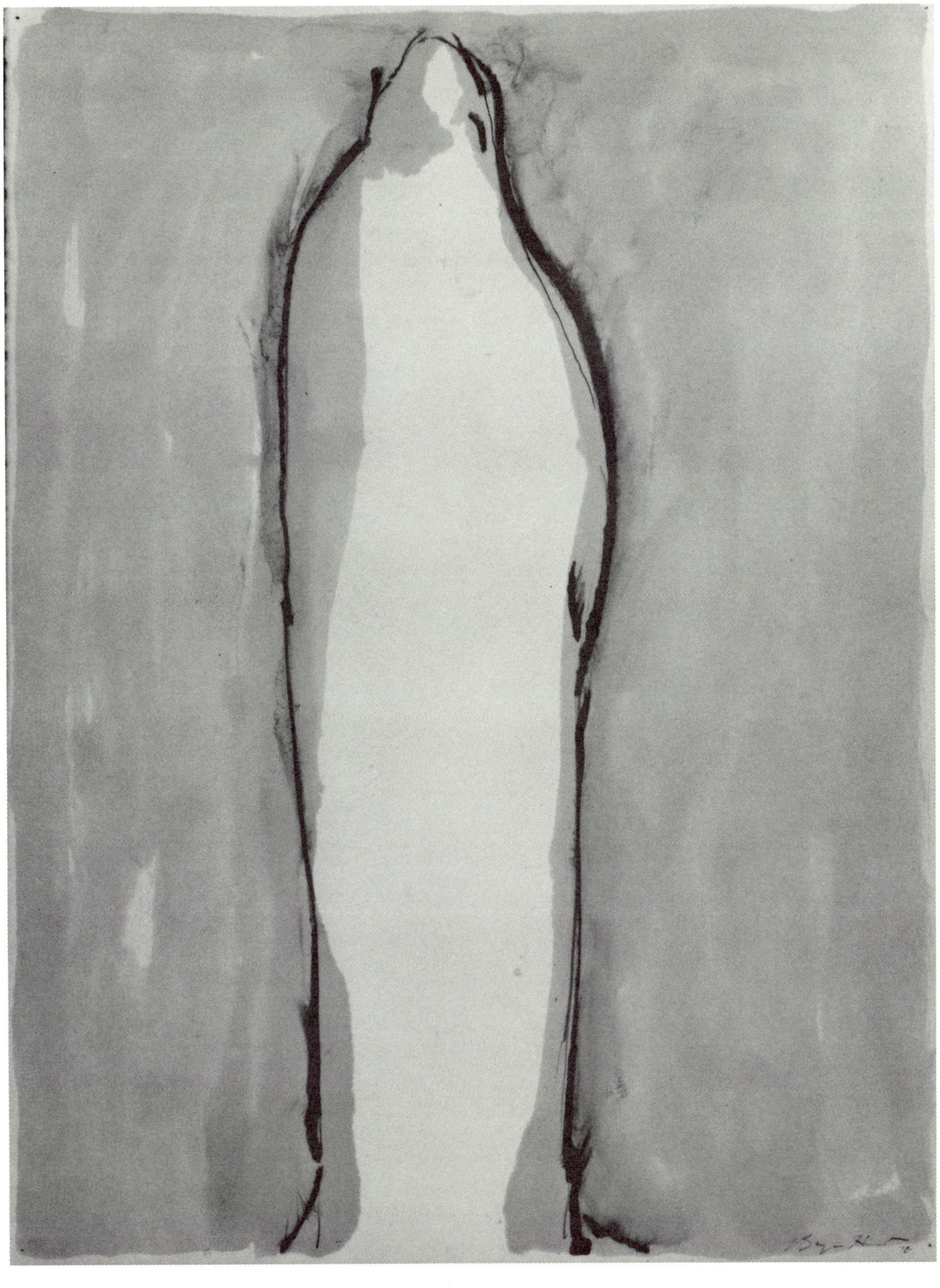

No. 10
***Balzac,** 1978*
graphite and linseed oil
on paper
30 x 22½"

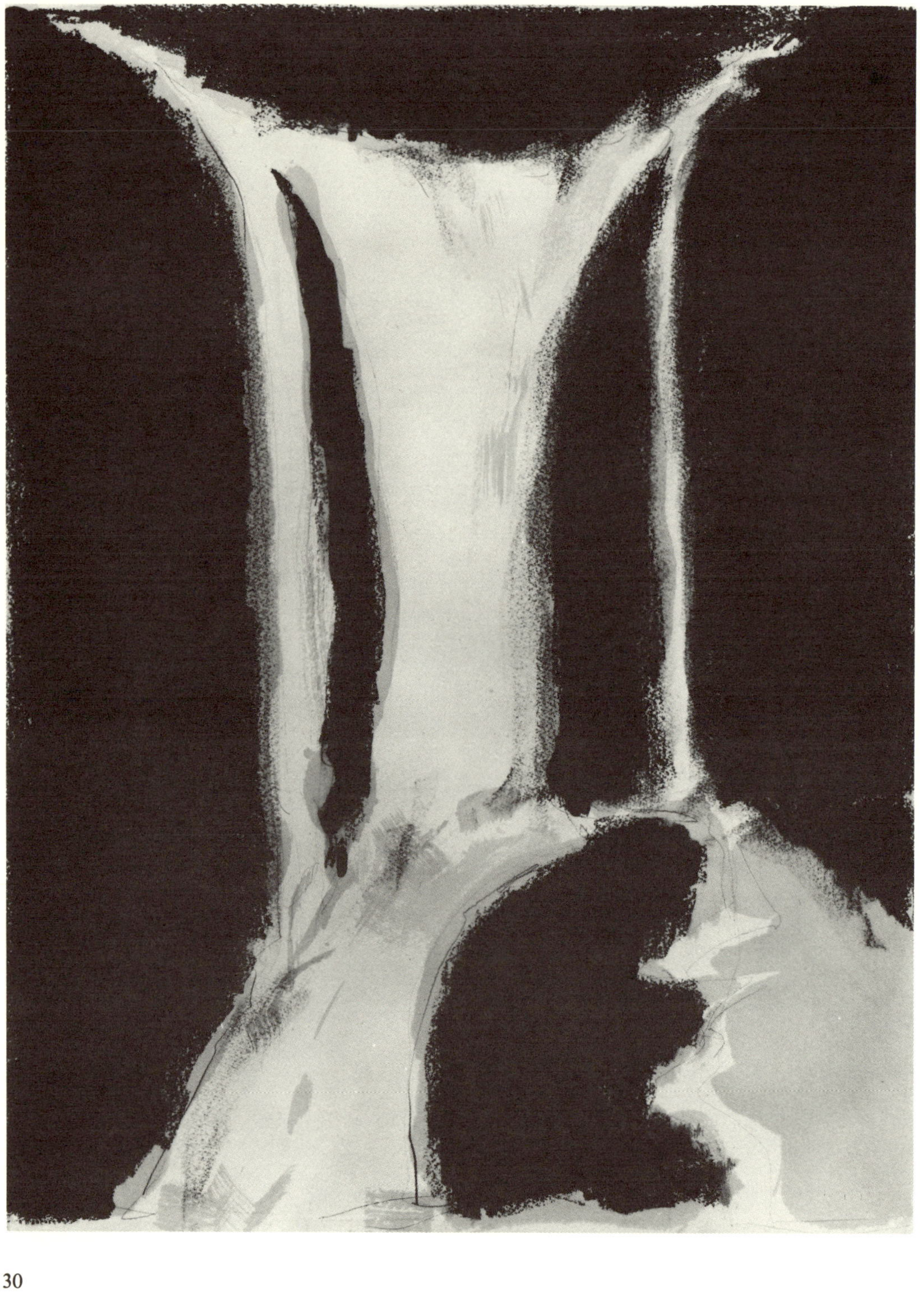

No. 27
***Throne Falls,** 1980*
graphite and linseed oil
on Arches paper
29½ x 22½"

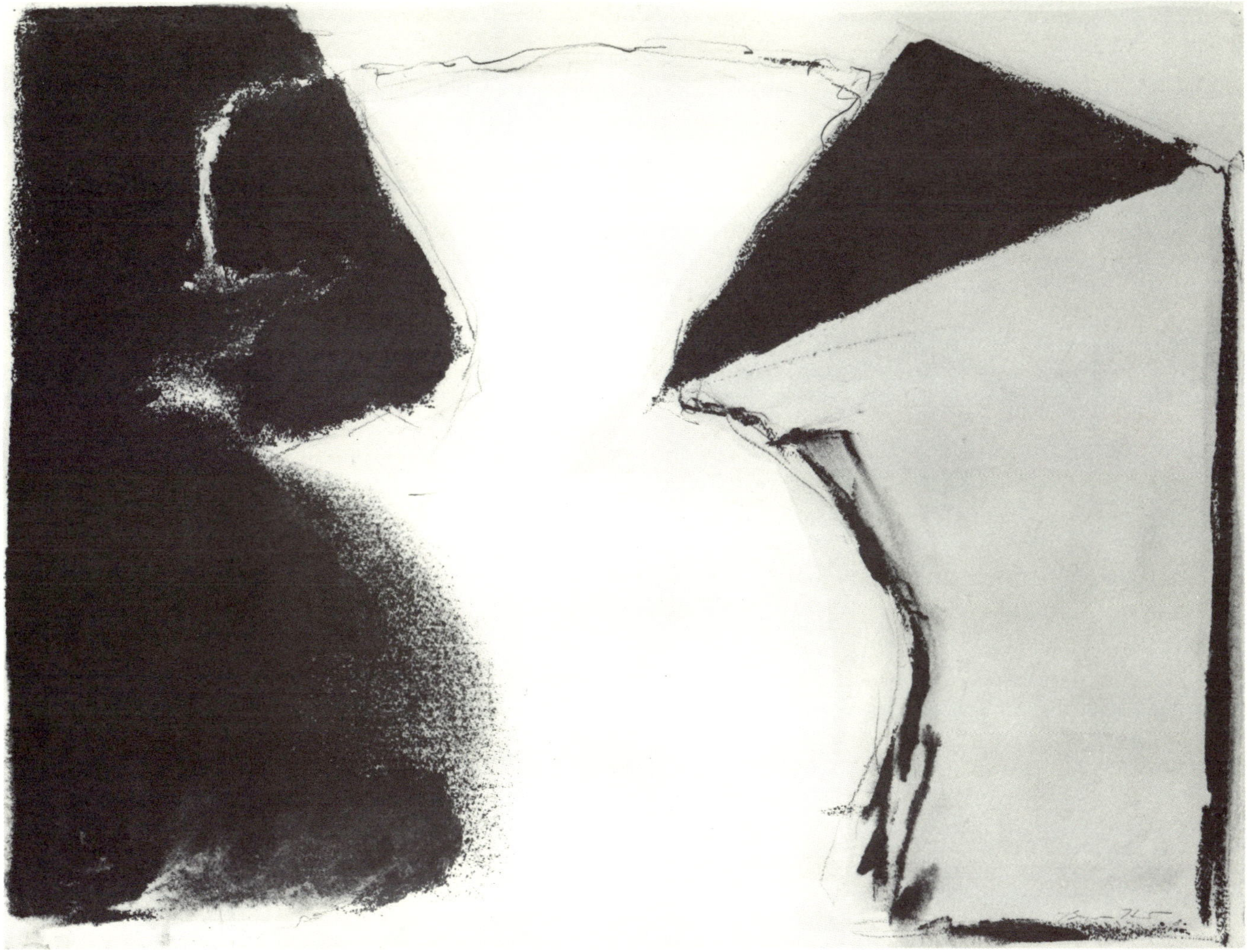

No. 24
The Dam, *1980*
graphite, linseed oil and conte crayon on Arches paper
23 x 29¾"

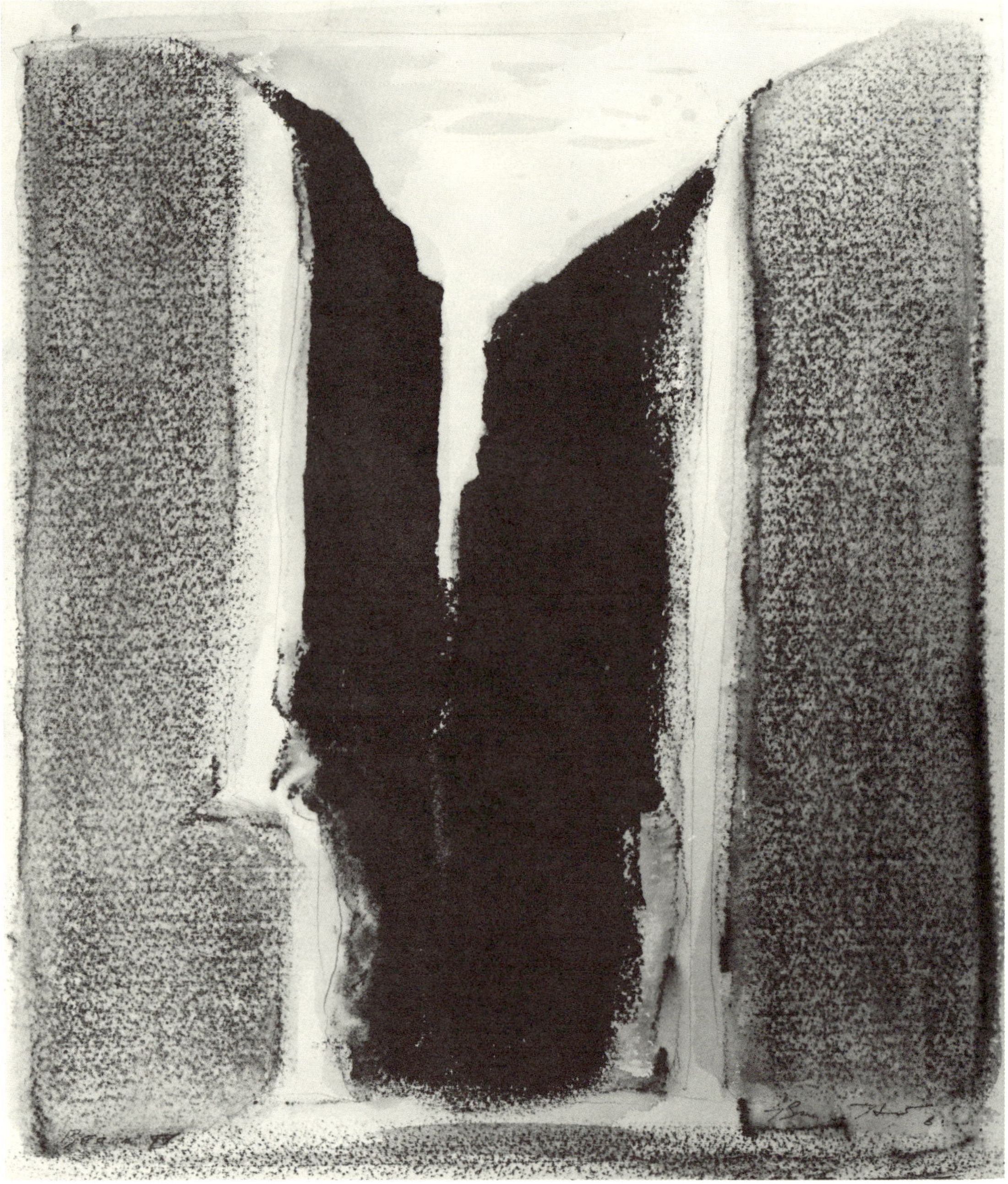

No. 29
Bequia IV, *1981*
graphite, linseed oil and watercolor on Arches paper
19 x 15¾"

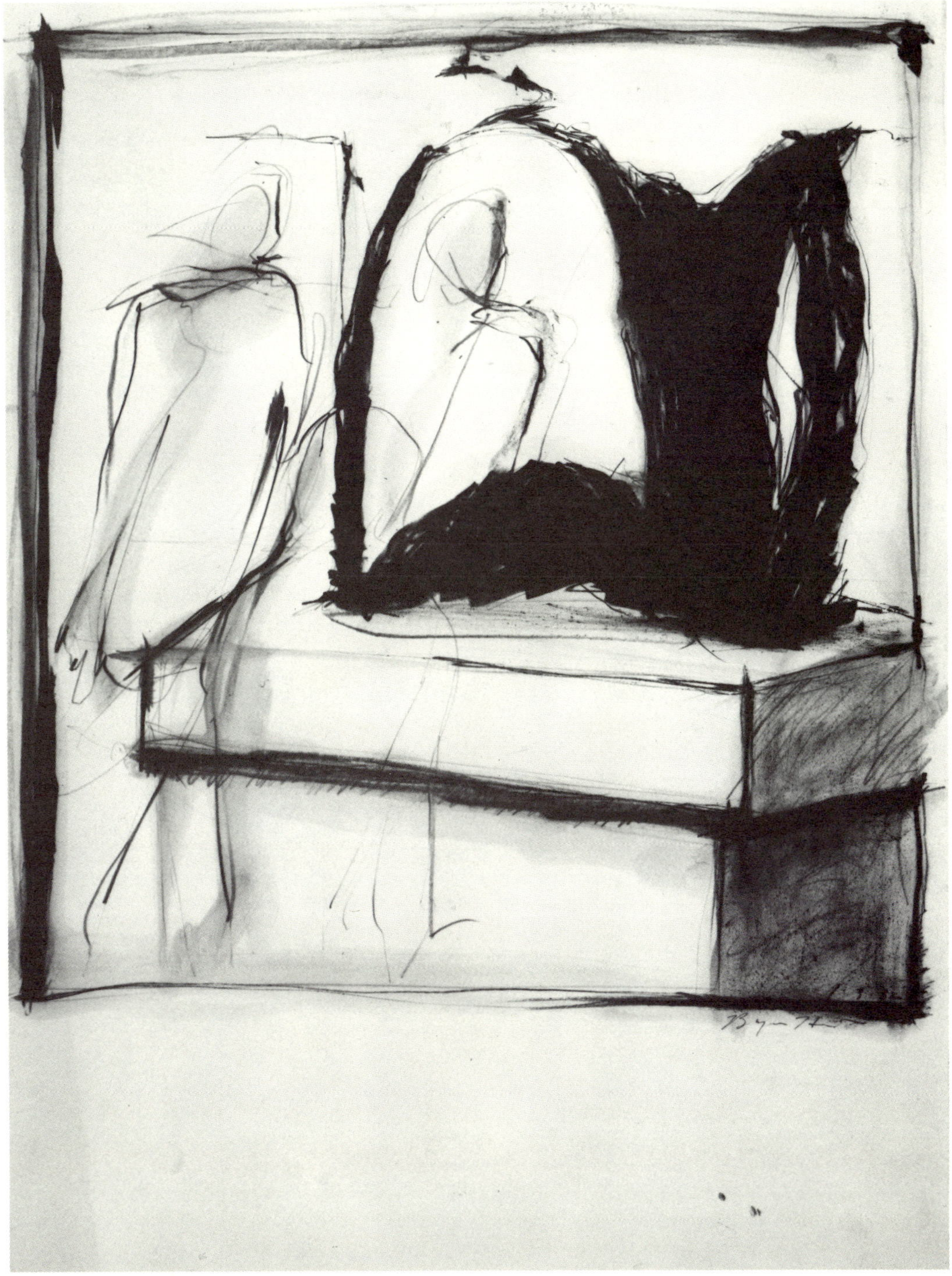

No. 37
***Conversation,** 1982*
graphite, linseed oil
and conte crayon on
Arches Satine paper
30¼ x 22½"

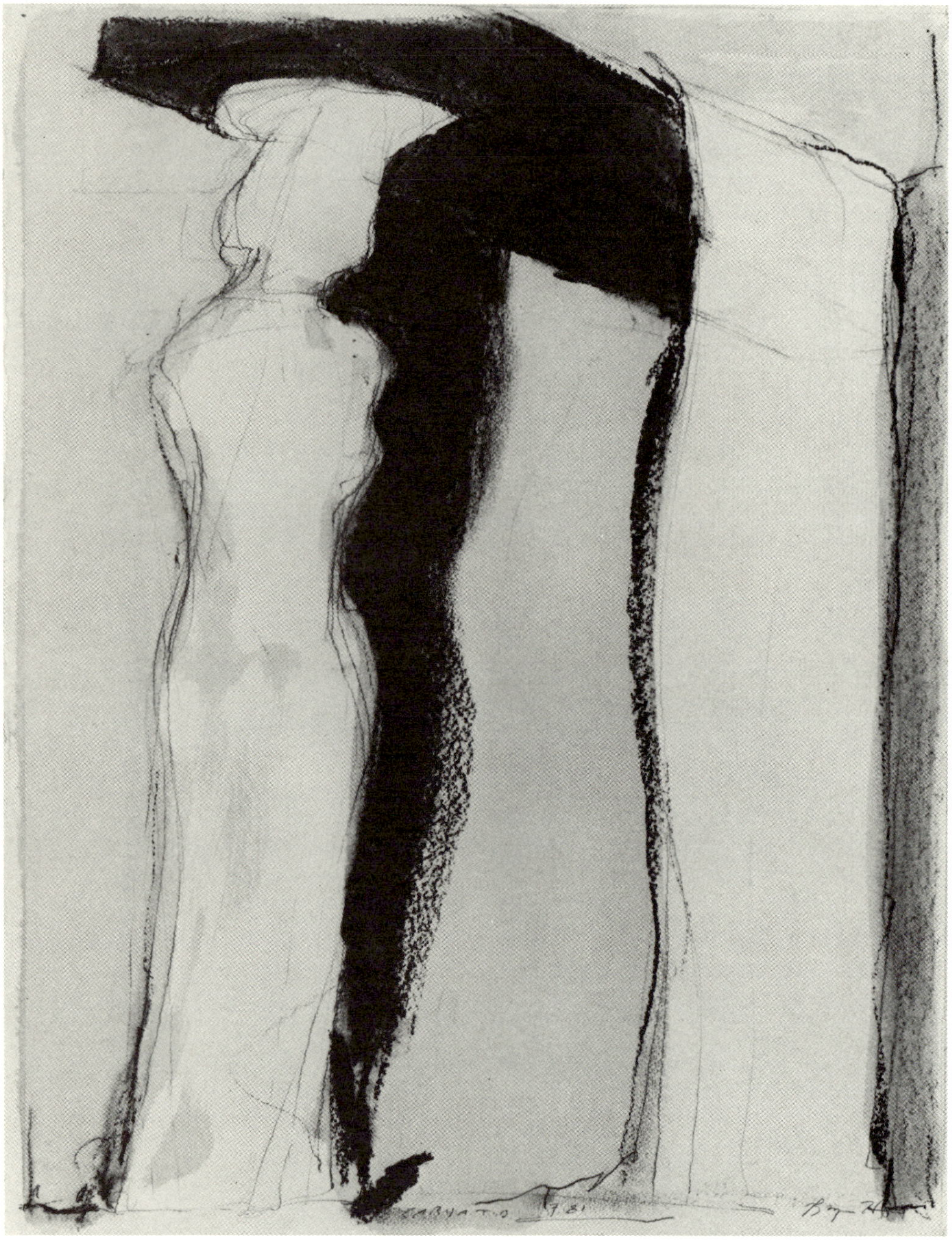

No. 30
***Caryatid II-Rhodean Series,** 1981*
graphite, linseed oil and conte crayon on Arches paper
24 x 18⅛"

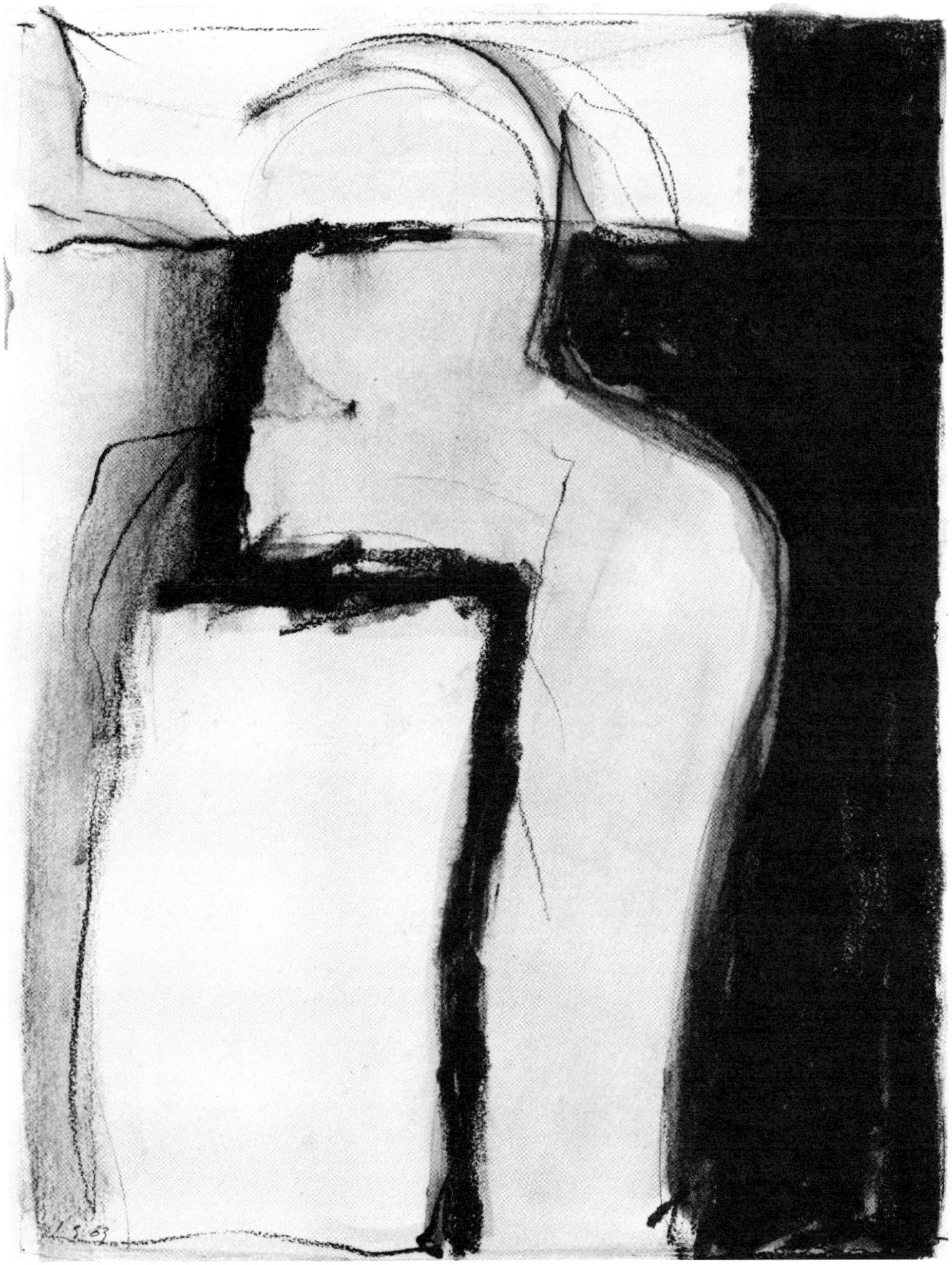

No. 45
***"1983,"**, 1983*
graphite, conte crayon and linseed oil on Arches paper
30 x 22⅞"

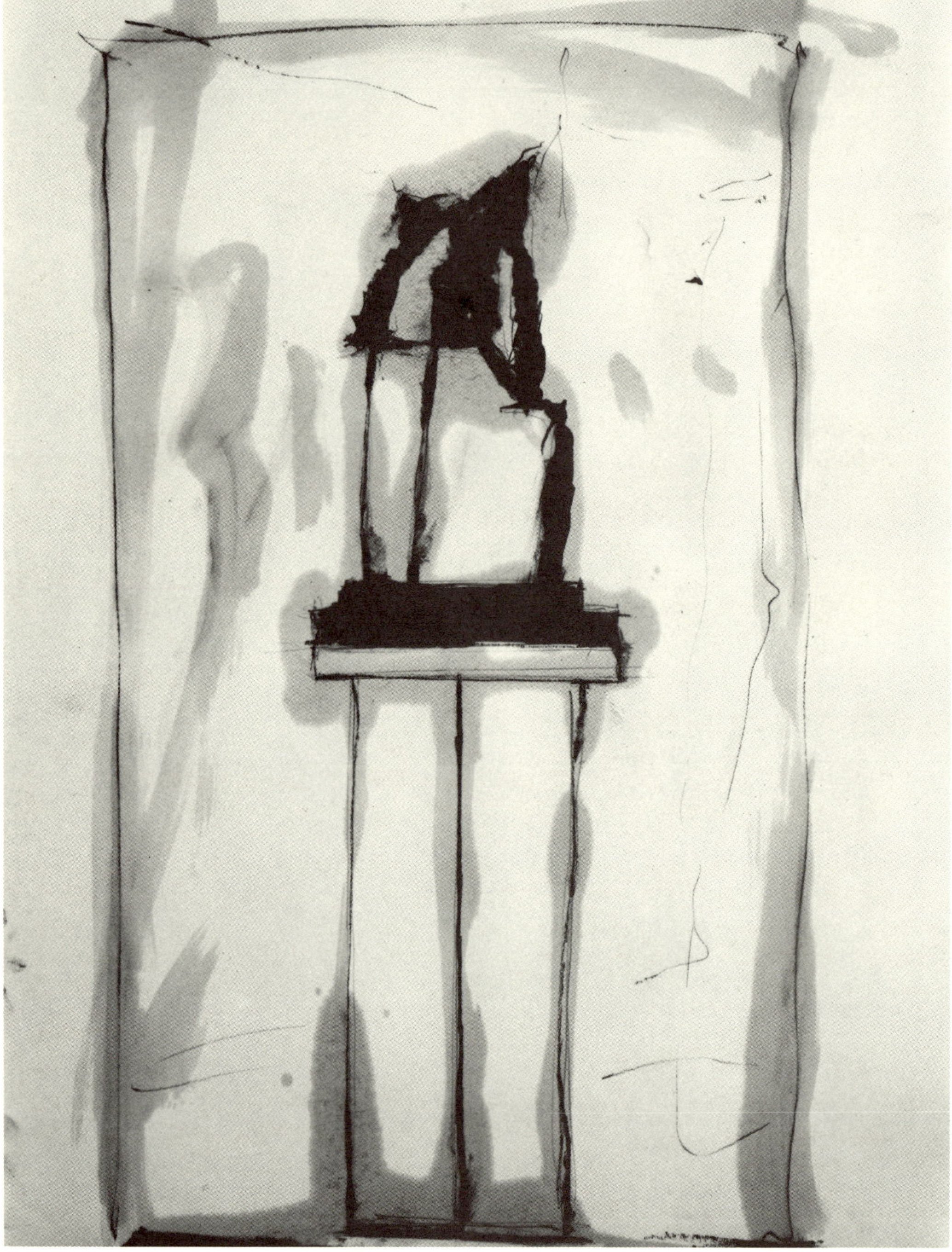

No. 47
***Roebling,** 1983*
graphite and linseed oil on paper
29¾ x 22"

BRYAN HUNT *Chronology*

1947:
Born June 7, Terre Haute, Indiana.

1957:
Family moves from Indiana to Tampa, Florida, approximately 100 miles from Cape Canaveral.

1959:
Watches rocket launchings at Cape Canaveral with his sixth grade class. This experience initiates Hunt's fascination with space exploration.

1967:
Attends University of South Florida, Tampa. Studies architecture and takes classes in engineering drawing.

1967-1969:
Works at Kennedy Space Center in a variety of positions ranging from mailboy to engineering aide.

1967-1968:
Visits Yosemite National Park during trip to California. Bridal Veil, Horse Tail, and Yosemite Falls make a lasting impression. Also travels to Europe. After losing his camera in Dover, England, substitutes drawing materials to record his travels. Of the many places he visits, cites the Parthenon as the most significant. These trips are the beginning of his use of travel to provide visual inspiration.

1969-1971:
Attends Otis Art Institute of Los Angeles. Receives Bachelor of Fine Arts degree and exhibits ceramic sculpture and paintings in student show. Establishes studio in Venice, California. In 1970, returns to Europe for three months.

1972:
Participates in Whitney Museum Artists Program in New York. Considers remaining in New York but returns to California.

1974:
Reads books on lighter-than-air transport which influence his style and re-kindle much of his excitement about space exploration. Builds his first sculpture, a realistic replica of the Empire State Building with a dirigible moored to its mast. Has earliest one-man exhibitions: *C. B. Hunt: Recent Works,* Institute for Art and Urban Resources at the Clocktower, New York; and *Bryan Hunt,* Jack Glenn Gallery, Corona del Mar, California.

1976:
Makes New York City his permanent home. Employed as a carpenter for a short time before beginning his association with the Blum Helman Gallery.

1977:
Establishes studio at 31 Great Jones Street. In conversation with astronaut Michael Collins, confesses his desire to use the space shuttle to launch one of his balsa and silk airships into orbit.

1978:
Included in the exhibition, *Young American Artists,* The Solomon R. Guggenheim Museum, New York. Commissioned to create a sculpture for Kaufmann House, *Falling Water,* Bear Run, Pennsylvania, by Frank Lloyd Wright. The result is a product of the artist's reaction to both the work of the architect, and this particular house and its environment. Titled *Bear Run,* the waterfall sculpture was created in plaster and cast in bronze.

1979:
Included in the *1979 Biennial Exhibition: Contemporary American Art,* Whitney Museum of American Art, New York.

1980:
Included in group exhibitions: *Twenty American Artists,* San Francisco Museum of Modern Art; and *Printed Art: A View of Two Decades,* The Museum of Modern Art, New York. Attends invitational artists' conference at Ponape, Micronesia, under sponsorship of Crown Point Press, and travels around the world.

1982:
Commissioned by The Museum of Modern Art to create *Conversations with Nature,* an artist's book composed of his photographs and drawings.

1983:
Moves studio to 9 White Street. Has one-man exhibition, *Gallery Six: Bryan Hunt,* Los Angeles County Museum of Art. Commissioned to create and install *Conductor II* on the site of the University Music Center, California State University, Long Beach.

One Man Exhibitions

1974:
The Clocktower Institute for Art and Urban Resources, New York
C.B. Hunt: Recent Works
October 17-November 16

Jack Glenn Gallery, Corona del Mar, California
Bryan Hunt
December 7-January 12, 1975

1975:
Palais des Beaux-Arts, Brussels
C. Bryan Hunt: 'Empire State/Graf' "Phobos" 'Universal Joint'
March 29-April 13

1976:
Daniel Weinberg Gallery, San Francisco
Bryan Hunt: Sculpture
July 10-August 7

1977:
Blum Helman Gallery, New York
Bryan Hunt: Sculpture
March 15-April 16

1978:
Blum Helman Gallery, New York
Bryan Hunt: New Sculpture and Drawings
April 17-May 13

Daniel Weinberg Gallery, San Francisco
Bryan Hunt: Sculpture and Drawings
July 11-September 2

Greenberg Gallery, St. Louis
Bryan Hunt: Sculpture
December 5-January 31, 1979

1979:
Blum Helman Gallery, New York
Bryan Hunt: Recent Sculpture
February 20-March 20

Bernard Jacobson Gallery, London
Bryan Hunt: Lakes • Waterfalls • Airships

Blum Helman Gallery, New York
Drawings

Galerie Bruno Bischofberger, Zurich
Bryan Hunt: Neue Werke
December 15-January 12, 1980

1980:
Margo Leavin Gallery, Los Angeles
Bryan Hunt
February 15-March 15

1981:
Akron Art Museum, Ohio
Bryan Hunt: Sculpture and Drawings
January 10-March 8

Blum Helman Gallery, New York
Bryan Hunt
May 5-June 6

Galerie Hans Strelow, Düsseldorf
Skulpturen und Zeichnungen
November 6-December 5

1982:
Daniel Weinberg Gallery, San Francisco
Bryan Hunt: Sculpture and Drawings
February 8-March 6

Bernier Gallery, Athens, Greece
Bryan Hunt Drawings
May 18-June 19

1983:
Blum Helman Gallery, 57th St., New York
Bryan Hunt
March 30-April 30

Blum Helman Gallery, Green St., New York
Bryan Hunt
April 2-May 14

Los Angeles County Museum of Art
Gallery Six: Bryan Hunt
April 21-June 19

Margo Leavin Gallery, Los Angeles
Bryan Hunt: Recent Sculpture & Drawings
April 23-May 28

Amerika Haus, Berlin
New Masters: Bryan Hunt
September 20-October 28

University Art Museum
California State University, Long Beach
Bryan Hunt: A Decade of Drawings
November 15-December 11

Group Exhibitions

1976:
Portland Center for the Visual Arts, Oregon
Via Los Angeles
January 8-February 8

Willard Gallery, New York
Selections
February 7-March 4

1977:
P.S. 1, Institute for Art and Urban Resources
Long Island City
Projects of the Seventies: New York Avant-Garde
October 9-November 6
Exhibition traveled through the Middle East and eastern Europe until 1979.

1978:
Daniel Weinberg Gallery, San Francisco
Up Against the Wall
January 28-February 25

Vassar College Art Gallery, Poughkeepsie, New York
Hunt, Jenney, Lane, Rothenberg, Shapiro
April 19-June 4

The Solomon R. Guggenheim Museum, New York
Young American Artists
May 5-June 6

Stedelijk Museum, Amsterdam
Made by Sculptors/door beedlhouwers gemaakt

1979:
The Katonah Gallery, Katonah, New York
Removed Realities—Aycock, Butterfield, Hunt, Shapiro
January 28-March 4

Whitney Museum of American Art, New York
1979 Biennial Exhibition: Contemporary American Art
February 14-May 1

The Renaissance Society at the University of Chicago, Illinois
Visionary Images
May 6-June 16

The Museum of Modern Art, New York
Selections from the Collection — Contemporary Sculpture
May 18-August 7

Whitney Museum of American Art, New York
Decade in Review
June 19-September 3

Daniel Weinberg Gallery, San Francisco
Bryan Hunt, Donald Sultan: Drawings
August 1-August 31

Hayden Gallery, Massachusetts Institute of Technology, Cambridge
Corners: Painterly & Sculptural Work
September 29-November 4

Galerie Hans Strelow, Düsseldorf
Junge amerikanische Kunst der achtziger Jahre

1980:
Bell Gallery, List Art Center, Brown University
Providence, Rhode Island
Invitational
February 2-February 24

The Museum of Modern Art, New York
Printed Art: A View of Two Decades
February 13-April 1

University Gallery, University of Massachusetts at Amherst
Sculpture on the Wall: Relief Sculpture of the Seventies
March 29-May 4

Daniel Weinberg Gallery, San Francisco
A Terrific Group Show
April 23-May 10

39th Venice Biennale
June 1-September 28

Indianapolis Museum of Art
Painting and Sculpture Today, 1980
June 24-August 17

San Francisco Museum of Modern Art
Twenty American Artists
July 24-September 7

Thomas Segal Gallery, Boston
Black and White
September 13-October 8

1981:
Whitney Museum of American Art, New York
1981 Biennial Exhibition
January 20-April 12

Hamilton Gallery, New York
Bronze
February 7-February 28

Contemporary Arts Museum, Houston
The Americans: The Landscape
April 4-May 31

Margo Leavin Gallery, Los Angeles
Cast, Carved and Constructed, An Exhibition of Contemporary American Sculpture
August 1-September 19

Akron Art Museum, Ohio
The Image in American Painting and Sculpture: 1950-1980
September 12-November 8

Blum Helman Gallery, New York
Bryan Hunt, Neil Jenney, Robert Moskowitz, Donald Sultan
September 16-October 10

Cleveland Museum of Art
Contemporary Artists
October 21-November 29

Sewall Art Gallery Rice University, Houston
Variants: Drawings by Contemporary Sculptors
November 2-December 19
Exhibition traveled to:
Art Museum of South Texas, Corpus Christi
December 31-January 28, 1982
Newcomb College, Tulane University, New Orleans
February 9-February 19, 1982
High Museum of Art, Atlanta, Georgia
March 26-May 2, 1982

Zabriskie Gallery, New York
E.R.A. Benefit Exhibition
November 17-November 24

1982:

Whitney Museum of American Art / Fairfield County
Stamford, Connecticut
Surveying the Seventies: Selections from the Permanent Collection of the Whitney Museum of American Art
February 11-March 31

Contemporary Arts Center, Cincinnati
Dynamix
March 11-April 17
Exhibition traveled to:
Sullivant Hall Gallery, Ohio State University, Columbus
September 6-October 17
Allen Memorial Art Museum, Oberlin College, Ohio
November 1-November 21
The Butler Institute of American Art
Youngstown, Ohio
December 6-January 9, 1983
University of Kentucky Art Museum, Lexington
January 15-February 20, 1983
Joslyn Art Museum, Omaha, Nebraska
March 19-May 1, 1983
Doane Hall Art Gallery, Allegheny College
Meadville, Pennsylvania
May 5-May 27, 1983

Freedman Gallery, Albright College
Reading, Pennsylvania
Landscape in Sculpture
March 15-April 18

Hayden Gallery, Massachusetts Institute of Technology, Cambridge
Great Big Drawings
April 3-May 2

Yale University Art Gallery, New Haven, Connecticut
Prints by Contemporary Sculptors
May 18-August 31

Larry Gagosian Gallery, Los Angeles
Works on Paper
May 22-June 26

The Art Institute of Chicago
74th American Exhibition
June 12-August 28

Blum Helman Gallery, New York
Drawings
June 23-July 30

Indianapolis Museum of Art
Painting and Sculpture Today, 1982
July 6-August 15

Fuller Goldeen Gallery, San Francisco
Casting: A Survey of Cast Metal Sculpture in the 80's
July 8-August 28

Newport Harbor Art Museum
Newport Beach, California
Shift: L.A./N.Y.
October 7-November 27
Exhibition traveled to:
Neuberger Museum, State University of New York at Purchase
October 9-December 24, 1983

The Museum of Modern Art, New York
Projects: Artist's Books
October 18-December 1

American Academy and Institute of Arts and Letters, New York
Hassam and Speicher Fund Purchase Exhibition
November 15-December 19

The Solomon R. Guggenheim Museum, New York
American Sculpture from the Permanent Collection
November 23-March 13, 1983

1983:

The Museum of Fine Arts, Houston
A Century of Modern Sculpture, 1882-1982
January 14, 1983-January 14, 1984

Daniel Weinberg Gallery, Los Angeles
Drawing Conclusions: A Survey of American Drawings: 1953-1983
January 29-February 26
Exhibition traveled to:
Daniel Weinberg Gallery, San Francisco
March 9-April 9

Castelli Graphics West, New York
Black and White: A Print Survey
January 29-February 26

Whitney Museum of American Art / Fairfield County
Stamford, Connecticut
Entering the Eighties
February 11-April 13

Whitney Museum of American Art at Phillip Morris, New York
Twentieth Century Sculpture: Presence and Process
April 8-May 11

McIntosh/Drysdale Gallery, Houston
Small Bronzes: A Survey of Contemporary Bronze Sculpture
April 12-May 14

San Francisco Museum of Modern Art
Bay Area Collects: A Diverse Sampling
April 21-June 26

Wave Hill, Bronx, New York
Bronze: Sculpture in the Landscape
May 19-September 30

Palais des Beaux-Arts, Brussels
Exhibition Auction of Contemporary Art
May 27-June 11

Whitney Museum of American Art, New York
Minimalism to Expressionism: Painting & Sculpture Since 1965 from the Permanent Collection
June 2-September 18

Margo Leavin Gallery, Los Angeles
Black & White
June 25-August 13

Ceolfrith Gallery, Sunderland Arts Centre
Sunderland, England
Drawing in Air: An Exhibition of Sculptors' Drawings, 1882-1982
July 11-August 20
Exhibition traveled to:
Glynn Vivian Art Gallery and Museum, Swansea
September 3-November 5
City Art Gallery and Henry Moore Study Centre, Leeds
January 13-February 19, 1984

Institute of Contemporary Art, Boston
Currents
September 13-November 27

Blum Helman Gallery, New York
Jan Groover, Bryan Hunt, Mel Kendrick
September 14-October 8

Nassau County Museum of Fine Art
Roslyn Harbor, New York
Sculpture: The Tradition in Steel
October 9-January 22, 1984

Velázquez Palace, Madrid
Tendencias en Nueva York
October 13-March 27, 1984

The Art Museum of The Ateneum, Helsinki
Ars '83 Helsinki
October 14-December 11

1984:

* Williams College Museum of Art
Williamstown, Massachusetts
Six in Bronze
January 15-February 20

Michele Redlich

*Projected at press time

Public Collections

Albright-Knox Art Gallery, Buffalo
Dallas Museum of Fine Arts
Des Moines Art Center
Frank Lloyd Wright Falling Water Conservancy,
  Kaufmann House, Bear Run, Pennsylvania
The Metropolitan Museum of Art, New York
Museum of Fine Arts, Boston
The Museum of Fine Arts, Houston
The Museum of Modern Art, New York
The Solomon R. Guggenheim Museum, New York
Vassar College Art Gallery, Poughkeepsie, New York
Whitney Museum of American Art, New York
Yale University Art Gallery, New Haven
Lehmbruck Museum, Duisburg, West Germany
Louisiana Museum of Modern Art,
  Humlebaek, Denmark
Stedelijk Museum, Amsterdam, The Netherlands
The University Art Museum, California State
  University, Long Beach

Exhibition List

1. *Erechtheum,* 1968
oil on paper
17 x 13¾″
Collection the artist

2. *Brooklyn Bridge Corner Drawing I,* 1974
graphite on vellum
drawing in two parts: 22⅝ x 19¾″; 22⅝ x 16⅛″
Collection John Duff, New York

* 3. *Ship Shape,* 1974
graphite and linseed oil on paper
24 x 87½″
Collection Sharon Haskell, New York

4. *Wall of China Drawing I,* 1974
graphite and linseed oil on paper
96 x 40″
Collection Mr. and Mrs. A. Charles Wilson
Beverly Hills

* 5. *Tower of Babel I (Pyramidal),* 1975
graphite and linseed oil on Arches paper
46½ x 29″
Private collection

* 6. *Myst,* 1977
graphite and linseed oil on Arches paper
30¼ x 22½″
Collection the artist

7. *Square,* 1977
graphite on paper
35½ x 39¾″
Collection the artist

* 8. *Twin Falls,* 1977
graphite and linseed oil on Arches apper
30¼ x 22½″
Collection Joseph A. Helman, New York

9. *Angel,* 1978
graphite and linseed oil on paper
22 x 5¼″
Collection Miani Johnson, New York

* 10. *Balzac,* 1978
graphite and linseed oil on paper
30 x 22½″
Private collection

* 11. *Black Falls IX,* 1978
graphite and linseed oil on paper
84¾ x 21¼″
Courtesy Yale University Art Gallery; purchased with the aid of funds from the National Endowment for the Arts and the Susan Morse Hilles Matching Fund

12. *Serpentine,* 1978
graphite and linseed oil on paper
22½ x 30″
Collection the artist

13. *The Balearic Studies II,* 1979
graphite, linseed oil and oilstick on Arches paper
5¼ x 7½″ each; series is comprised of seven drawings
Collection the artist

14. *Bastion,* 1979
graphite and linseed oil on paper
30 x 22½″
Collection Joseph A. Helman, New York

15. *Black Falls XXV,* 1979
graphite and linseed oil on paper
84 x 21″
Collection Alan Shayne, Los Angeles

16. *Horizon Falls,* 1979
graphite and linseed oil on paper
23 x 29½″
Collection Ms. Ames Cushing, Los Angeles
Courtesy Margo Leavin Gallery, Los Angeles

17. *Horizon Falls,* 1979
graphite and linseed oil on Arches paper
22½ x 30″
Private collection

18. *Line Drawing XV,* 1979
graphite and linseed oil on paper
84 x 21″
Private collection, Los Angeles
Courtesy Margo Leavin Gallery, Los Angeles

19. *The Meeting,* 1979
graphite and linseed oil on Arches paper
22½ x 30″
Private collection

20. *Ship Shape,* 1979
graphite, linseed oil and oilstick on Arches paper
14⅛ x 19¾″
Private collection

21. *Untitled,* 1979
graphite and linseed oil on Arches paper
22 x 30″
Courtesy Margo Leavin Gallery, Los Angeles

22. *Cycladic Dream,* 1980
graphite and linseed oil on paper
29¼ x 23″
Private collection

* 23. *Cubit Quarry,* 1980
graphite and linseed oil on paper
24 x 71¾″
Private collection

* 24. *The Dam,* 1980
graphite, linseed oil and conte crayon on Arches paper
23 x 29¾″
Collection Peter Freeman

25. *Secret Place,* 1980
graphite and linseed oil on Arches paper
29½ x 23″
Private collection

26. *Sneak Preview,* 1980
ink and graphite on Arches paper
29¾ x 23″
Collection the artist

* 27. *Throne Falls,* 1980
graphite and linseed oil on Arches paper
29½ x 22½″
Private Collection, Boston

28. *To R.S.,* 1980
graphite and linseed oil on paper
30 x 22½″
Collection Calvin Tomkins, New York

* 29. *Bequia IV,* 1981
graphite, watercolor and linseed oil on Arches paper
19 x 15¾″
Courtesy Albright-Knox Art Gallery, Buffalo,
New York, James G. Forsyth Fund, 1981

* 30. *Caryatid II - Rhodean Series,* 1981
graphite, linseed oil and conte crayon on Arches paper
24 x 18⅛″
Collection the artist

* 31. *Limn Drawing,* 1981
graphite, linseed oil and copper leaf on paper
28 x 84″
Private collection

32. *Lost Head Falls,* 1981
graphite, linseed oil and conte crayon on paper
14 x 19¾″
Private collection

33. *Untitled,* 1981
graphite, linseed oil and conte crayon on Arches paper
19¼ x 14¼″
Private collection

34. *Whale Island,* 1981
graphite, watercolor and oilstick on
Arches Torchon paper
19¼ x 16″
Private collection

* 35. *Calyx - Aphrodite - Hermes,* 1982
graphite, linseed oil and conte crayon on paper
8¾ x 6⅜″
Private collection

36. *Caryatid,* 1982
graphite, linseed oil and conte crayon on Arches paper
17½ x 12¾″
Private collection

* 37. *Conversation,* 1982
graphite, linseed oil and conte crayon on
Arches Satine paper
30¼ x 22½″
Private collection

* 38. *Converse Passage,* 1982
graphite, linseed oil and conte crayon on paper
84½ x 34⅛″
Collection Blum Helman Gallery, New York

39. *Doors Series,* 1982
graphite, linseed oil and conte crayon on paper
84½ x 34″
Collection Warren Adelson, New York

* 40. *Grecian Study,* 1982
graphite, linseed oil and conte crayon on paper
8¾ x 6⅜″
Private collection

* 41. *Proserpine,* 1982
graphite, linseed oil and conte crayon on paper
85 x 35″
Private collection
Courtesy Margo Leavin Gallery, Los Angeles

42. *Separation I,* 1982
graphite, conte crayon and linseed oil on paper
30 x 22⅞″
Collection Robertson Colman & Stephens
San Francisco
Courtesy Margo Leavin Gallery, Los Angeles

43. *Ascension,* 1983
graphite, linseed oil and conte crayon on Arches paper
30 x 22½″ each; series is comprised of four drawings
Courtesy Blum Helman Gallery, New York

44. *Crux,* 1983
graphite, linseed oil and conte crayon on paper
30 x 22¾″
Collection Jonathan Leaver, New York

* 45. *"1983,"* 1983
graphite, linseed oil and conte crayon on Arches paper
30 x 22⅞″
Collection Douglas S. Cramer, Los Angeles

46. *Plutarch's Lives,* 1983
graphite, linseed oil and conte crayon on paper
84 x 35″
Collection Steve Martin, Los Angeles

* 47. *Roebling,* 1983
graphite and linseed oil on paper
29¾ x 22″
Private collection

* 48. *Study for Conductor II,* 1983
graphite and conte crayon on paper
and vellum with Polaroid photograph
24 x 18″
Collection University Art Museum
California State University, Long Beach

* indicates illustration

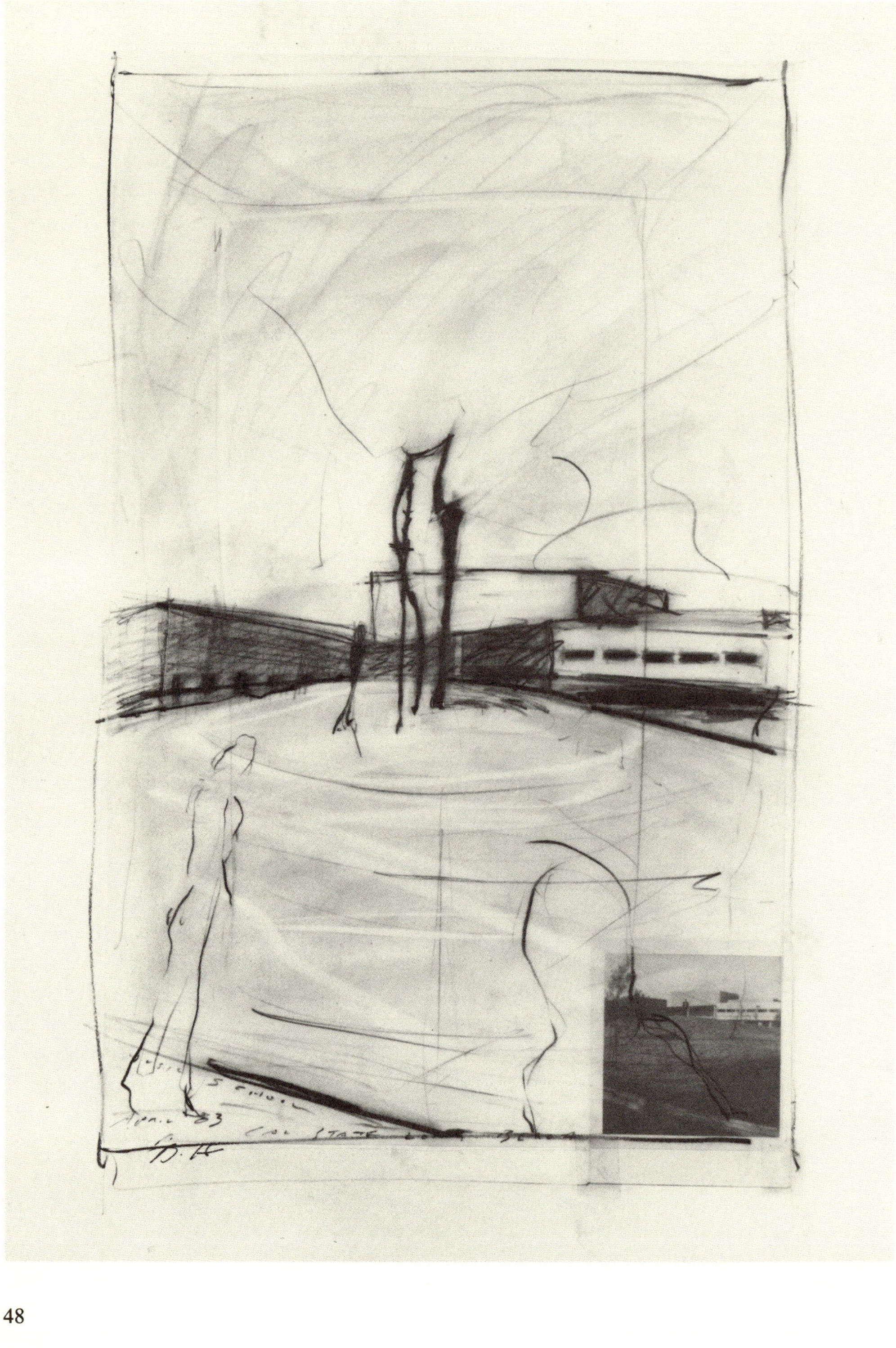

No. 48
Study for Conductor II, *1983*
graphite and conte crayon on paper and vellum with Polaroid photograph
24 x 18"

Afterword

In Consideration of Sculpture

In Recognition of the concurrent commissioning of Bryan Hunt's sculpture ***Conductor II*** *for the grounds of the University Music Center.*

Monumental sculpture has long been an important component of the visual milieu of CSU Long Beach. In 1965 the campus was the site of the first International Sculpture Symposium to be held on a college campus. Organized by Art Department Professor Kenn Glenn, the symposium was also one of the earliest formal explorations of the merger of art and technology. Eight world renowned sculptors were invited to be in residence in Long Beach and materials, facilities, and technical staff from neighboring industrial concerns were made available to them. The sculptures which were created became the nucleus of a continuously growing collection installed throughout the 320 acre campus. Together with this new work by Bryan Hunt, other additions of special note include *Window Wall for Cal State Long Beach* by Robert Irwin (gift of the artist to the University Art Museum and retained from the 1975 Museum Studies Class Exhibition, *A View Through),* and *In Irons* by Guy Dill (a gift of Marcia and Frederick Weisman).

As is the case with most publicly held collections, the patronage of individuals, corporations, and public agencies has played an essential role in the acquisition of each work in the CSULB sculpture collection. The commissioning of *Conductor II* was made possible by an Art in Public Places grant from the National Endowment for the Arts awarded to the University Art Museum and matched by support from the CSULB Fine Arts Affiliates and the Louise Carlson Cultural Fund. As the new University Music Center neared completion, the Fine Arts Affiliates, led by then co-Presidents Sheri and Seldon Beebe, followed by President Roy Jarvis, along with Fine Arts Dean Jane Milley, sought a fitting way to commemorate the completion of this magnificent addition to the campus. It was decided that since the new music buildings were sited in a heretofore undeveloped area of the campus, it would be most appropriate to commission a work of sculpture. Such a commission would not only enhance the site, it would also contribute to the existing sculpture collection and serve to further integrate the new complex into the visual fabric of the University.

Following established NEA and University procedures, Bryan Hunt was offered, and accepted, the commission. Meanwhile the Affiliates began the challenging task of raising the matching funds required to bring their dream to fruition. The response of the Long Beach community was both swift and gratifying and the Affiliates soon reached their goal. A generous contribution from the Louise Carlson Cultural Fund completed the matching requirements of the grant.

Just as the availability of books in the library, the presentation of musical and theatrical performances, and opportunities to take part in the social and political life of the University contribute to the richness and variety of the education available to every student attending CSU Long Beach, the Monumental Sculpture Collection and the University Art Museum exhibitions and programs contribute to the development of visual literacy in every student. However, because of the cost and complexity of museum programs and acquisitions, university museums around the country increasingly must appeal to off-campus patrons for support for these activities. The Long Beach community has continually demonstrated its willingness to provide this support for the visual arts on the CSU Long Beach campus and it is with pleasure that the Museum and the School of Fine Arts acknowledges this commitment to excellence and community service.

Jane K. Bledsoe

BRYAN HUNT
Sculpture: Materials and Processes

Like artists throughout history who have chosen materials and processes which best serve their ideological needs, Bryan Hunt combines a variety of materials and numerous sculptural processes to achieve a highly personal idiom. In the tradition of Auguste Rodin, Hunt pays close attention to detail and texture. He works on a human scale which makes evident the artist's "hand." "I work within the realm of my reach because I want that personal contact — the larger the scale . . . , the less connected I would be."[1] The artist first gained recognition in the early 1970s with a continuing series of airship sculptures — sleek, cerebral, dirigible-shaped forms. Further additions to this body of work include lakes, quarries and waterfalls — naturalistic, rough-textured, earthy forms in bronze.

The construction of the airships is a meticulous and meditative process. A complex frame composed of balsa ribs and numerous thin bands of lightweight spruce determines the shape of the airship. This wooden frame is covered with silk or silk paper and is in turn covered with gold, silver or copper leaf. Light reflected from the metal-leafed surface creates a glowing sensation. Horizontally penetrating into space, the airships appear to defy gravity (fig. 7). "The less physical weight the airship seems to support, the more it looks like it's floating, so it has a psychological presence based on this characteristic of weightlessness."[2]

In contrast to the complex inner structure of the airships, the waterfalls are formed over simple welded steel armatures.[3] Traditionally, an armature functions as a hidden support structure over which the artist molds and shapes his material. Hunt's reasons for incorporating the armature into his work are not simply functional, but philosophical, in that he also visualizes his artistic activity of the last ten years as an armature. "Everyone is interested in building up a level of mystery and expression on top of it."[4] In this context, he has created a series of very linear sculptures which are, in

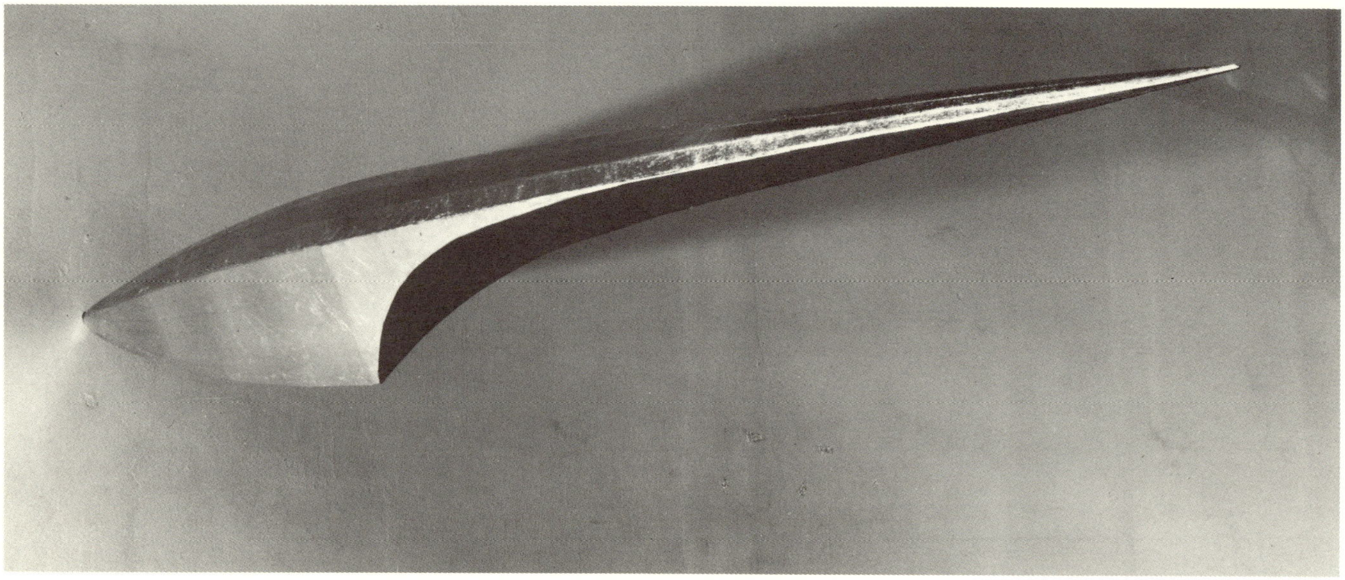

Figure 7. *Bryan Hunt,* ***1986,*** *1980, mixed media. Photograph courtesy of Blum Helman.*

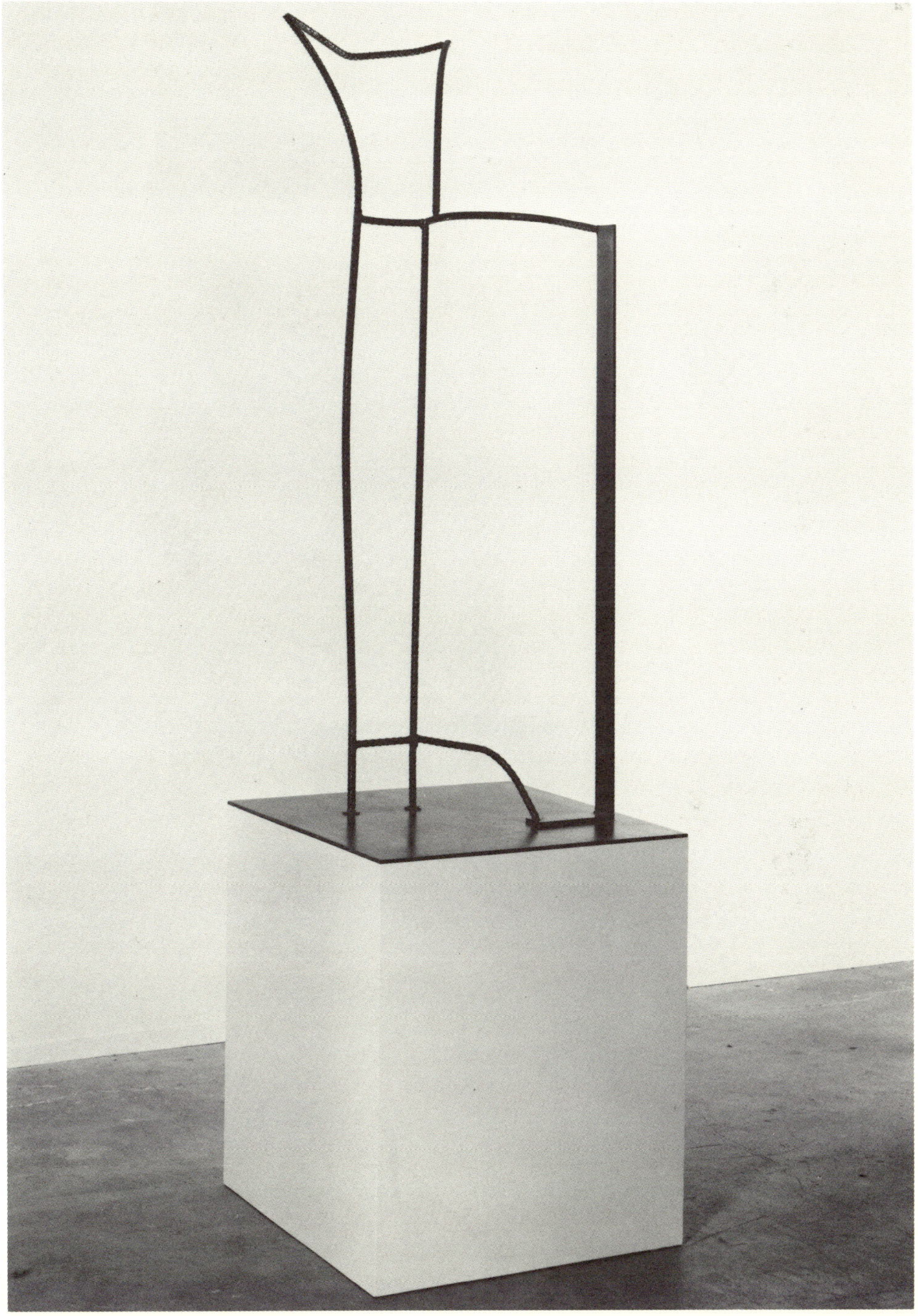

Figure 8. *Bryan Hunt,* ***Linear II,*** *1981, welded steel. Photograph courtesy of Blum Helman.*

fact, steel armatures(fig. 8). He describes these works as "drawing in space" because of the similarity they bear to a portion of his work on paper.[5]

The issue of gravity played a fundamental role in the emergence of modern sculpture, especially in the works of artists such as Rodin and Degas, whose figures are depicted in a state of suspended movement.[6] In the same manner, Hunt's methods have evolved in part from an examination of gravity. He cites Rodin's *Monument to Balzac* (fig. 9), which he describes as a thrusting abstract form with an incredible dynamic force, as having been particularly influential in the development of his own work.[7] Hunt imitates Rodin's upward force in the waterfalls which depict, as if temporarily reversing the action of gravity, the arrested motion of water (fig. 10).

This effect is achieved by initially tilting the armature for the vertical waterfall on its side. The surface is then built with layers of plaster and plaster-soaked cloth. Plaster the consistency of heavy cream is poured in a directional manner in order to create the illusion of water under gravitational pull. Before the plaster sets, Hunt often dips his fingers into the surface, forming lines which exaggerate the flow of the plaster/water. Once the plaster hardens, the piece is returned to its upright position. Using woodcarver's tools, Hunt carves the surface edges, creating added expressionist passages. The marks cut into the plaster thrust upward, denying gravity and playing with light.[8] A recent modification of this technique is the application and modeling of small amounts of plasticene (an oily synthetic clay) onto the plaster surface. The most linear works are created by shaping only plasticene directly onto the armature.

In the Minimalist tradition, Bryan Hunt reduces his work to essential form. "I like the idea of having a simplified shape, one that can be understood easily, and yet suggest geometric or even mathematical properties."[9] Although Hunt's focus on gestural surfaces is a sharp denial of Minimalist principles, his lakes and quarries best exemplify his interest in Minimalist reduction (fig. 11).[10] These otherwise flat-appearing horizontal forms are stripped of their earthen containers and become textured three-dimensional forms, therefore differentiating them from Minimal sculpture. Hunt builds and carves the bottom surfaces of the lake

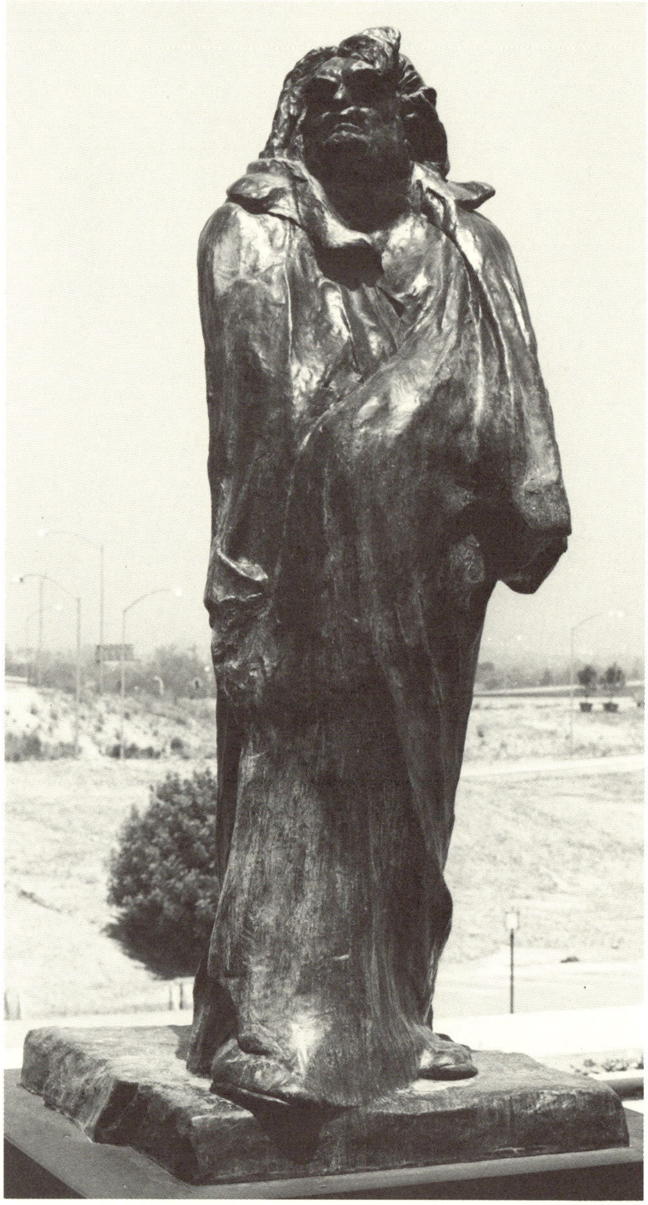

Figure 9. *Auguste Rodin,* ***Monument to Balzac,*** *1891-1898, bronze. Photograph courtesy of The Norton Simon Foundation, Pasadena, California.*

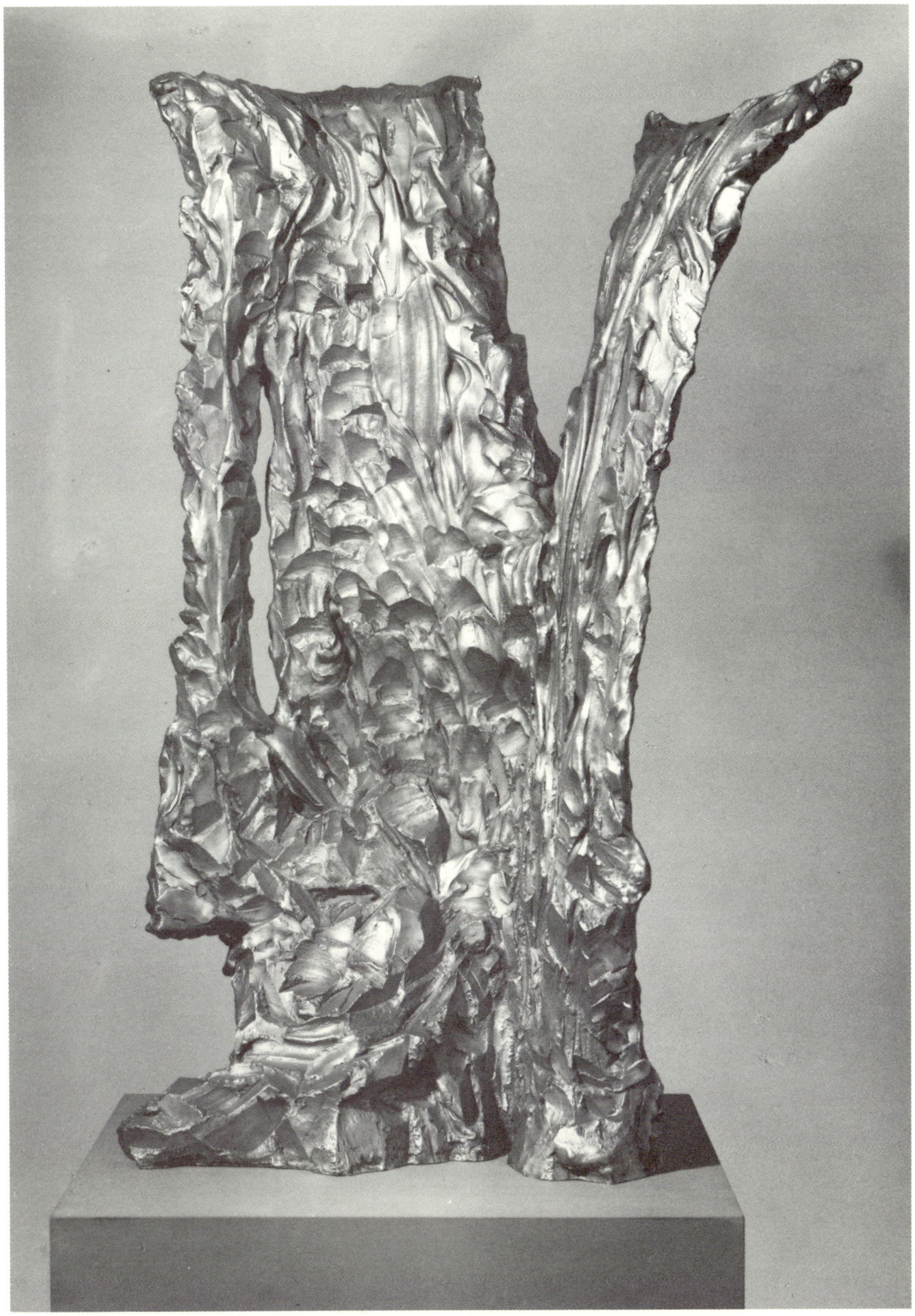

Figure 10. *Bryan Hunt,* ***Bastion,*** *1981, bronze. Photograph courtesy of Blum Helman.*

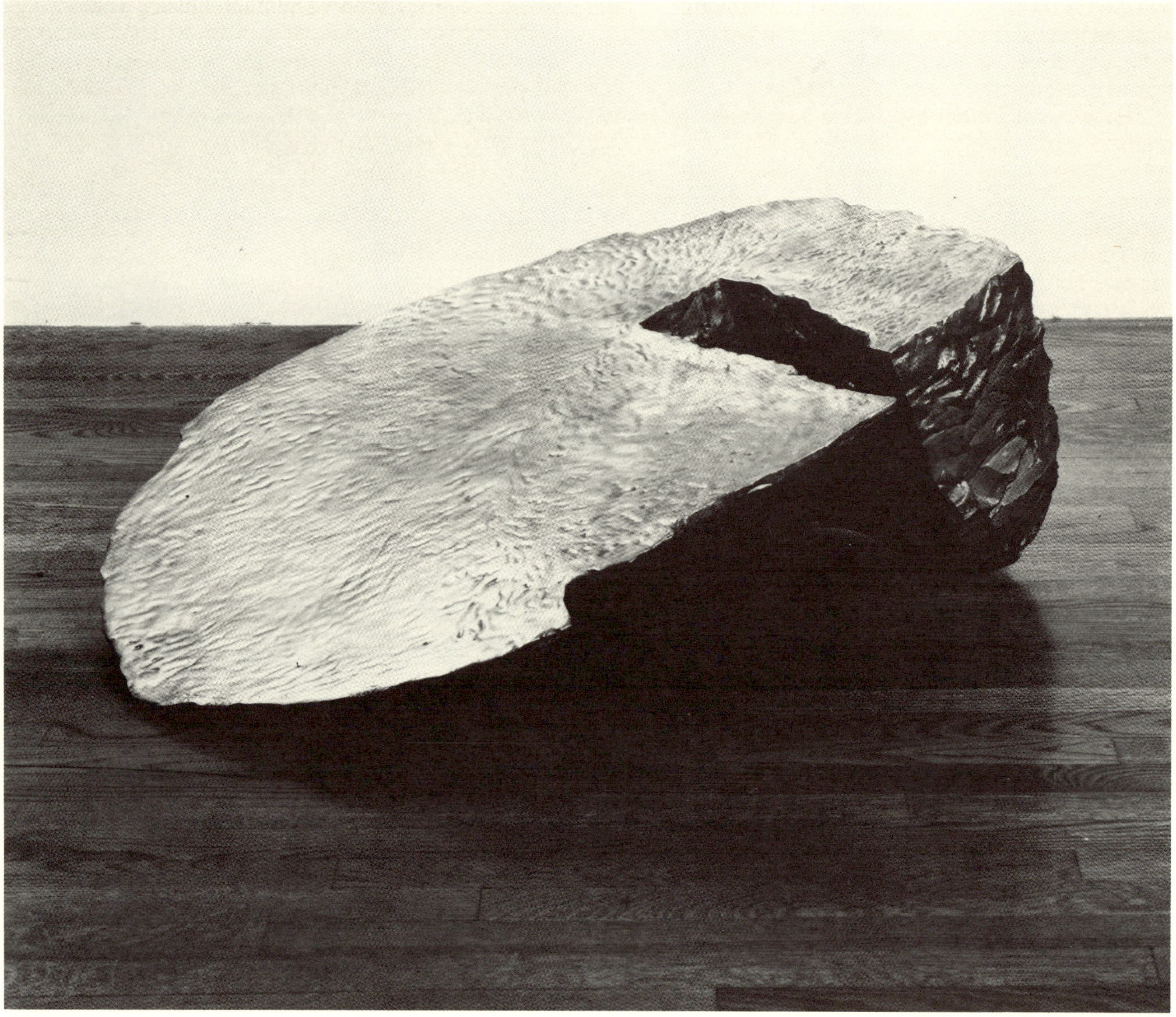

Figure 11. *Bryan Hunt, **Cubit Quarry,** 1979, bronze. Photograph courtesy of Blum Helman.*

and quarry pieces from plaster. Wave patterns are attained through the application of a thin layer of wax to the upper, flat surface. This layer is then etched and heated to achieve the desired rippled effect.

Hunt considers molten metal to be the most appropriate material to represent the frozen action of water. He and other artists such as Robert Graham, Joel Shapiro and Lynda Benglis have contributed to a recent resurgence of interest in bronze sculpture. Sculptors of the 1960s and early 1970s abandoned bronze, which was considered to be uneconomical, bourgeois, conservative, timid, traditional. Many of the materials they used, however, were impermanent. Artist/critic Wade Saunders suggests that many of these artists are now returning to bronze out of a desire to achieve immortality, and that the rising number of public commissions in recent years — bronze being a durable exterior material — may also be a contributing factor.[11]

Bronze casting is a complex and time-consuming process. Although other casting methods exist, the lost-wax process is most often employed when a work of solid metal is desired. A rubber mold is made from the original plaster and a wax replica is then imbedded within a plaster investment or casing. Heated over a period of days or weeks, the wax drains from vents cut into the investment. At last, the molten bronze is poured into the hollow cavity once occupied by the wax replica. After the metal has cooled the plaster investment is removed to reveal the bronze cast. The number of casts from a single plaster is a matter of choice by the artist. Hunt usually destroys the original plaster once an edition of three to four pieces is cast.[12] The finishing touch is the application of a patina or coloring agent. Hunt consults with the foundry craftsmen to determine the most appropriate patina for each piece. Black is a favorite of his, however he often leaves the bronze in its natural state. Following patination, the sealer is applied to the completed bronze sculpture. Finally, whether one is attracted to the classic sensuality of Hunt's bronzes or the sleek elegance of his airships, the aesthetic qualities we perceive in Bryan Hunt's sculpture are a result of the materials and processes he has chosen and the intimate relationship that exists between the artist and his sculptural technique.

Christie A. Collins

Notes

[1] Robin White, "Bryan Hunt: Interview," ***View*** *(Oakland, California: Crown Point Press), April 1980, p. 11.*

[2] Ibid., p. 10.

[3] Ibid., p. 22

[4] Dupuy Warrick Reed, "Bryan Hunt," ***Flash Art,*** *October/November 1981, p.50.*

[5] Bryan Hunt Interview, California State University, Long Beach, February 9, 1983.

[6] William Tucker, "Gravity: Rodin, Degas," ***Studio International*** *186 (July/August 1973): 25.*

[7] White, p. 12.

[8] Reed, p. 49.

[9] Linda Shearer, "Bryan Hunt," in ***Young American Artists*** *(New York: Solomon R. Guggenheim Museum, 1978), p. 32.*

[10] Jeanne Siegel, "Bryan Hunt," ***Arts Magazine*** *51 (May 1977): 20.*

[11] Wade Saunders, "Hot Metal," ***Art in America*** *68 (Summer 1980): 88.*

[12] Bryan Hunt, February 9, 1983

Selected Bibliography: Bryan Hunt

Books:

Hunt, Bryan. *Conversations with Nature.* New York: The Museum of Modern Art, 1982.

Johnson, Ellen H., ed. *American Artists on Art from 1940 to 1980.* New York: Harper & Row Publishers Inc., 1982.

Krantz, Les, ed. *The New York Art Review.* Forward by Leo Castelli. New York: McMillan Publishing Company, 1982.

Catalogues:

Armstrong, Thomas; McCarthy, Gerard and Phillips, Lisa. *Twentieth Century Sculpture: Process and Presence.* New York: Whitney Museum of American Art at Phillip Morris, 1983.

1979 Biennial Exhibition, Whitney Museum of American Art. New York: Whitney Museum of American Art, 1979.

1981 Biennial Exhibition, Whitney Museum of American Art. New York: Whitney Museum of American Art, 1981.

Carr, Carolyn Kinder. *The Image In American Painting and Sculpture: 1950-1980.* Preface by I. Michael Danoff. Akron, Ohio: Akron Art Museum, 1981.

Castleman, Riva. *Printed Art: A View of Two Decades.* New York: The Museum of Modern Art, 1980.

Cathcart, Linda. *The Americans: The Landscape.* Houston, Texas: Contemporary Arts Museum, 1981.

Davies, Hugh M. *Sculpture on the Wall: Relief Sculpture of the Seventies.* Amherst, Massachusetts: University Gallery, University of Massachusetts at Amherst, 1980.

Dippel, Rini, and Beijeren, Geertuan van. *Door beeldhouwers gemaakt* [Made by sculptors]. Amsterdam: Stedelijk Museum, 1978.

Drawing in Air: An Exhibition of Sculptors' Drawings, 1882-1982. Sunderland, England: Sunderland Arts Centre, Ceolfrith Gallery, 1983.

Elsen, Albert. *Casting: A Survey of Cast Metal Sculpture in the 80's.* San Francisco, California: Fuller Goldeen Gallery, 1982.

Ferrulli, Helen and Yassin, Robert A. *Painting and Sculpture Today: 1982.* Indianapolis, Indiana: Indianapolis Musem of Art, 1982.

Field, Richard S. and Rosenfield, Daniel. *Prints by Contemporary Sculptors.* New Haven, Connecticut: Yale University Art Gallery, 1982.

Halbreich, Kathy. *Corners.* Cambridge, Massachusetts: Hayden Gallery, Massachusetts Institute of Technology, 1979.

Hinson, Tom E. *Contemporary Artists.* Cleveland, Ohio: The Cleveland Museum of Art, 1981.

Hopkins, Henry T. *20 American Artists.* San Francisco: San Francisco Museum of Modern Art, 1980.

Kline, Katy. *Great Big Drawings.* Cambridge: Hayden Gallery, Massachusetts Institute of Technology, 1982.

McShine, Kynaston. *Selections from the Collection: Contemporary Sculpture.* New York: The Museum of Modern Art, 1979.

Morrin, Peter. *Hunt, Jenney, Lane, Rothenberg, Shapiro.* Poughkeepsie, New York: Vassar College Art Gallery, 1978.

Phillips, Lisa. *Surveying the Seventies: Selections from the Permanent Collection of the Whitney Museum of American Art.* Stamford, Connecticut: Whitney Museum of American Art/ Fairfield County, 1982.

Ratcliff, Carter. *Visionary Images.* Chicago, Illinois: The Renaissance Society at the University of Chicago, 1979.

————. *Bryan Hunt.* New York & Los Angeles: Blum Helman Gallery and Margo Leavin Gallery, 1983.

Rossen, Susan. *74th American Exhibition.* Essay by Anne Rorimar. Chicago, Illinois: The Art Institute of Chicago, 1982.

Russell, Laura W. *Variants: Drawings by Contemporary Sculptors.* Introduction by Esther de Viecsey. Houston, Texas: Sewall Art Gallery Rice University, 1981.

Schimmel, Paul. *Shift: LA/NY.* Newport Beach, California: Newport Harbor Art Museum, 1982.

Shearer, Linda. *Young American Artists.* New York: The Solomon R. Guggenheim Museum, 1978.

Stearns, Robert. *Dynamix.* Cincinnati, Ohio: Contemporary Arts Center, 1982.

Yassin, Robert. *Painting and Sculpture Today: 1980.* Indianapolis, Indiana: Indianapolis Museum of Art, 1980.

Articles:

Bowsher, John. "An Essence of Landscapes." *Artweek,* June 4, 1983, p. 16.

Brown, Christopher. "Bryan Hunt Sculptures." *Artweek,* August 26, 1978, pp. 1, 16.

Buettner, Stewart. "Six Los Angeles Artists." *Artweek,* January 31, 1976, p. 16.

Cebulski, Frank. "Scales of Nature." *Artweek,* February 27, 1982, p. 5.

Crossley, Mimi. "Review: The Americans: The Landscape." *The Houston Post,* April 12, 1981, p. 10 AA.

Danoff, Michael I. "Bryan Hunt: Sculpture and Drawings." *Dialogue: The Ohio Arts Journal,* January/February 1981, p. 51.

DeSantis, Tullio Francesca. "Modern Sculpture: Albright Show Offers Unique Perspectives." *Reading Eagle,* March 21, 1982, pp. 57, 63.

Dickson, Joanne A. "Bryan Hunt: Evidence of Things Unseen." *Artweek,* July 31, 1976, p. 5.

Eisler, Colin. "Prints by Contemporary Sculptors." *Art Journal,* Fall 1980, pp. 247-48.

Foster, Hal. "Reviews from New York, Las Vegas, Los Angeles, San Francisco, Cologne, and Rome." *Artforum,* September 1981, pp. 77-8.

Frank, Peter. "New York Review: Bryan Hunt." *ARTnews,* October 1978, p. 178.

Freeman, Nan. "The Magnitude of Drawing." *Art New England,* April, 1982.

Friedrichs, Yvonne. "Dem Wasser eine feste Form: Bryan Hunt in der Galerie Streblow[sic]/ Erstmals in Deutshland" [Giving Water Stable Form: Bryan Hunt at the Strelow Gallery/First time in Germany]. *Rheinische Post,* November 27, 1981.

"Gallery Six: Bryan Hunt." *Los Angeles County Museum of Art Members Calendar,* May, 1983; np.

Glenn, Constance W. "Artist's Dialogue: A Conversation With Bryan Hunt." *Architectural Digest,* March 1983, pp. 68-74.

Glueck, Grace. "Artists Conference Alights at a South Seas Island." *The New York Times,* February 24, 1980.

————. "2 — Gallery Shows Are Catching On." *The New York Times,* April 8, 1983, sec. C, pp. 1, 5.

Hale, Nike. "Young Artists at Guggenheim." *Art World,* May 18/June 16, 1978, pp. 1, 6-7.

Kalil, Susie. "The American Landscape — Contemporary Interpretations." *Artweek,* April 25, 1981, pp. 9-10.

Kramer, Hilton. "Bronze Makes A Comeback." *The New York Times,* February 8, 1981, pp. 33, 42.

————. "Sculptors Who Triumph in Bronze." *The New York Times,* May 24, 1981, pp. 25, 35.

Larson, Kay. "Between a Rock and a Soft Place." *New York Magazine,* June 1, 1981, p. 56.

McDonald, Robert. "The World Simply Seen." *Artweek,* August 25, 1979, p. 4.

Muchnic, Suzanne. "A 'Cast' of 21 at Leavin Gallery." *Los Angeles Times,* August 28, 1981, sec. 6, p. 2.

————. "The Galleries." *Los Angeles Times,* May 6, 1983, sec. 6, p. 13.

Nahum, Katherine. "Hayden exhibit sheds light into corners." *The Newton Times,* October 17, 1979, p. 11.

Perrone, Jeff. "Reviews New York: Bryan Hunt." *Artforum,* Summer 1977, p. 68.

Phillips, Deborah C. "New York Reviews: Bryan Hunt." *ARTnews,* September 1981, p. 233.

Poett, James. "A Pail of Water Without a Pail." *The Village Voice,* March 1977, p. 89.

Reed, Dupuy Warrick. "Bryan Hunt." *Arts Magazine,* April 1979, p. 7.

————. "Bryan Hunt." *Flash Art,* October-November 1981, pp. 49-50.

Rickey, Carrie. "Reviews New York." *Artforum,* May 1979, p. 58.

Saunders, Wade. "Hot Metal." *Art In America,* Summer 1980, pp. 87-95.

Schwartz, Ellen. "New York Reviews: Bryan Hunt." *ARTnews,* Summer 1979, p. 182.

Schwarze, Dirk. "Unbefangene Kunst: Hans Strelow zeigt junge Amerikaner [Unencumbered Art: Hans Strelow shows young artists]. *Rheinische Post,* January 5, 1980.

Siegel, Jeanne. "Bryan Hunt." *Arts Magazine,* May 1977, p. 20.

Smith, Roberta. "Biennial Blues." *Art In America,* April 1981, pp. 92-101.

Taylor, Robert. "Do Corners Have an Intrinsic Value?" *Boston Sunday Globe,* October 17, 1979, p. D2.

Tennant, Donna. "CAM exhibit samples contemporary landscapes." *Houston Chronicle,* April 16, 1981, sec. 3, p. 8.

————. "The Americans: The Landscape." *Houston Chronicle, Texas Magazine,* April 26, 1981, sec. 3, p.8.

Tomkins, Calvin. "The Art World — Boom." *The New Yorker,* December 22, 1980, p. 78-80.

Van Houten, David. "Brian [sic] Hunt." *Artweek,* January 11, 1975, pp. 3-4.

Wilson, William. "The Galleries." *Los Angeles Times,* February 22, 1980, sec. 6, p. 8.

Wohlfert, Lee. "Young Artists New Yorkers Are Talking About." *Town & Country,* September 1980, pp. 199-207.

Wortz, Melinda. "Los Angeles: Hieroglyphic Umbrellas." *ARTnews,* May 1980, p. 141.

————. "The LA/NY Shift: For Some Artists, The Fast Lane Heads East." *ARTnews,* January 1983, pp. 67-71.

Zimmer, William. "Art Review — Whitney Biennial." *The Soho Weekly News,* February 11, 1981.

————. "Building Materials." *The Soho Weekly News,* March 8, 1979, p. 53.

————. "Hunt's Points." *The Soho Weekly News,* May 13, 1981, p. 51.

————. "The Peaks in Review." *The Soho Weekly News,* February 11, 1981, pp. 27-28.

————. "Wall Feat." *The Soho Weekly News,* December 6, 1979, pp. 20, 71, 76.

Interviews:

Becker, Robert. "Bryan Hunt." *Interview,* January 1982, pp. 52-54.

Brooks, Valerie F. "Arts Extra." Radio Broadcast, July 15, 1983. WBAI-FM, New York.

Cumming Paul. "A Conversation About Drawing." *Drawing,* Vol. 5, No. 3, September/October, 1983, pp. 49-55.

Hunt, Bryan. University Art Museum, California State University Long Beach. Interview, February 9, 1983.

Hunt, Bryan. University Art Museum, California State University Long Beach. Interview, April 25, 1983.

Hunt, Bryan. Margo Leavin Gallery, Los Angeles. Lecture, April 26, 1983.

White, Robin. "Bryan Hunt: Interview." *View,* Vol. III, No. 1, April 1980, pp. 5-23.

Recordings:

Word of Mouth, Vision #4. Oakland, California: Crown Point Press and the Museum of Conceptual Art, San Francisco, 1980.

C. Michelle Betty

Selected Bibliography: General Sources

Battock, Gregory. *Minimal Art: A Critical Anthology.* New York: E.P. Dutton, 1968.

Brown, Elizabeth Ann. "Sculptors' Drawings." *Arts Magazine,* June 1981, p. 22.

Eisler, Colin, ed. *Sculptors' Drawings Over Six Centuries 1400-1950.* New York: Agrinde Publications, 1981.

Fong, Wen. *Summer Mountains.* New York: The Metropolitan Museum of Art, 1975.

Gowing, Lawrence. *Matisse.* New York: Oxford University Press, 1979.

Hutter, Heribert. *Drawing: History and Technique.* Translated by D.S.J. Thomson. New York: McGraw-Hill Book Company, 1966.

Johnson, Ellen H. *Modern Art and the Object.* New York: Harper & Row Publishers, 1976.

Judd, Donald. "Specific Objects." *Contemporary Sculpture,* in *Arts Yearbook 8.* New York: The Art Digest, Inc., 1965.

Lee, Sherman E. *Chinese Landscape Painting.* Revised edition. New York: Harper & Row Publishers, Inc., 1962.

Leymarie, Jean Genevieve Monnier, and Rose, Bernice. *Drawing: History of an Art.* New York: Rizzoli, 1979.

Longstreet, Stephen. *The Drawings of Rodin.* Alhambra, California: Borden Publishing Company, 1965.

Mendelowitz, Daniel Marcus. *Drawing.* New York: Holt, Rinehart and Winston, 1967.

Padovano, Anthony. *The Process of Sculpture.* Garden City, New York: Doubleday and Company, 1981.

Phillips, Deborah C. "Where Painting and Sculpture Meet," *ARTnews,* June 1980, p. 248.

Read, Herbert. *A Concise History of Modern Sculpture.* New York: Praeger Publishers, 1971.

Rosenberg, Harold. "Defining Art," Reprint from *The New Yorker,* February 25, 1967, in *Minimal Art: A Critical Anthology,* ed. Gregory Battock. New York: The Art Digest, 1965.

Schuler, Josef Egon, and Hansler, Rolf, eds. *Great Drawings of the Masters.* Translated by Gillian Brydone. New York: G.P. Putnam's Sons, 1963.

Strachan, Walter John. "The Sculptor and His Drawings." *Connoisseur.* July 1974, pp. 186-190.

————. *Towards Sculpture: Drawings and Maquettes from Rodin to Oldenburg.* Boulder, Colorado: Westview Press, 1976.

Tucker, William. "Gravity: Rodin, Degas." *Studio International,* July/August 1973, pp. 25-29.

Photo Credits

Photography by: Roy M. Elkind, figs. 7, 10; Roger Gass, fig. 8; David Behl, fig. 11; Joseph Szaszfai, No. 11; Bill Jacobson, Nos. 3, 8, 10, 37, 47; Jon Abbott, Nos. 23, 24, 27; David Lubarsky, No. 30; Jerry L. Thompson, No. 45, Mark Chamberlain, BC Space, Laguna Beach, California, No. 48; ©Arnold Newman, New York, portrait of Bryan Hunt. All Photographs courtesy of Blum Helman Gallery, New York, with the exception of: Harry N. Abrams, New York, fig. 1; *The Print Collector's Newsletter* and Aaron Siskind, fig. 2; Wesleyan University Press, Middletown, Connecticut, fig. 3; ©Robert A. M. Stern, fig. 4; The National Gallery of Canada, Ottawa, fig. 5; The Norton Simon Foundation, Pasadena, California, fig. 9; Yale University Art Gallery, New Haven, Connecticut, fig. 11; Albright-Knox Art Gallery, Buffalo, New York, No. 29.

Colophon

This catalogue was designed in Santa Ana by Kirsten Jacobs Whalen; type set in Times Roman by Queen Beach Printers, Inc., Long Beach, California; lithographed in an edition of 1,500 on 100# Sonata Kidskin by Queen Beach Printers, Inc.